Aum Sri Uchchhishta Maha Ganapathaye Namah:

# Yogi, Thithi, Karana and Indu Lagna

Tirupur S. Gopalakrishnan

**Translated by Haraprasad R**

ISBN 979-8-89322-600-3

Sri Uchchhishta Maha Ganapathaye Namah!
Submitted at the Lotus feet of my Living God Guruji

**Shri. Tirupur. S. Gopalakrishnan**

# Dedication

I offer my humble prayers
To
My Parents
Who have
Parented Me
And
Raised me up
Considering my development
As their own
Bless me Dad
Bless me Mom

# CONTENTS



A.   Indu Lagna (IL)

B.   Indu Lagna Calculation

C.   More on Indu Lagna

D.   Example Charts for Calculation of Indu Lagna (IL).

E.   Indu Lagna in Perspective

F.   Indu Lagna Yoga(s) – Few Snippets

G.   Rules

H.   Few Additional Pointers & Summary in Brief

# Contents

# Contents

# PRAYER

Let us submit our prayers to

Our mother

Our Father

Those who were our preceptors and pedagogue till now by touching their lotus feet

Our family deity

Our tutelary God

Our chosen God

Guardian deity

Special/specific deities of the residential town

Let mystics, saints, gurus, spiritual heads, eminent astrologers, the five elements, nature, stellar constellation, the zodiac, the planets, and omnipresent power bless us.

Let our word, act, and deeds not hurt or hinder people's progress.

Let peace prevail with all.

Sri Uchchhishta Maha Ganapathaye Namah!

Sri Uchchhishta Maha Ganapathaye Namah!

Sri Uchchhishta Maha Ganapathaye Namah!

I always offer my prayers along the above lines at the start of every class.

I bestow this prayer to everybody

# PRAYERS TO PRECEPTOR

I hereby submit my humble prayers

To my father who is also my first preceptor in astrology

Late Shri. N. Selvarasu Pillai for giving me

love, education, pleasure, enlightenment, and knowledge

To my Guru Late Shri. Guru Ramasubbu

To my Guru who leads me in absentia Late
Shri. K. S. Krishnamurthy (K.S.K)

I submit my humble prayers to all saints and spiritual Gurus,
Rishis, and astrological fraternity.

My greetings to my fellow astrologers.

Seeking the blessings of all
– Tirupur S. Gopalakrishnan (Tirupur GK)

Sri Uchchhishta Maha Ganapathaye Namah!

# THANKS NOTE

This book was originally published in Tamil and received attention and appreciation from all.

I submit my humble thanks to my mentor and guide of all time Dr. K Nataraj P.hd., (Astro), Oddanchathiram.

I take this opportunity to thank Guruji Shri L. Duraiswamy, Headmaster (Retd) and honorary President of Gurunathar Nadi Astrology Centre.

I would like to thank the Admin of GK Foundation Ms. Aswini K. Thangalakshmi – Sankarankoil for her efforts in the propagation of my astrological thoughts to all through our Foundation.

I also take this opportunity to express my sincere thanks to:

Mr. Sankar and Mrs. Tamizharasi Sankar – Tirupur

Sri D. Balakrishnan – Axe Oil, Chennai,

Sri R. Sakthivel – Ayyappa Label,

Sri P. R. Selvaganesh – Bangalore for being the reason for my many books in many languages,

My well-wisher Sri Aditya Guruji – Chennai.

Sri. Haraprasad R, Chennai for translating this book into English.

I must also thank

Sri S. Suresh – Coimbatore,

Sri B. Senthilkumar – Tirupur, all the GK Astro Admin-executives for their tireless support to me.

My sincere thanks to the management, executives, and staff of "Notion Press' for bringing up this book in a fitting manner.

I convey my heartfelt thanks and blessings to everyone.

– Tirupur S. Gopalakrishnan, (Tirupur GK)<br>
9842220903<br>
Gkastro.tirupur@gmail.com

# AUTHOR'S FOREWORD

The original Tamil version of this book was the first one released after the inauguration of the gurukul at Tirupur. This is an outcome of a long period of gestation of research—like that of a mother delivering a child. The probing Q&A sessions with my students have helped in its evolution with a refreshing outlook.

I am an avid follower of Panchanga and my experience and application of its elements with the individual horoscopes has resulted in this compilation. However, in order to protect the privacy of the Natives, I have just restricted my observations on crucial planetary impacts without complete disclosure.

This book is an important milestone in my Astro Journey. The concepts of Indu Lagna, Karana, Yogi – Avayogi are covered in good detail. Besides that, Thithi Shunya and the impact of the planets in Thithi Shunya are also explained in depth. Thithi primarily plays a significant role in progeny matters, Nakshatra in day to day practical life and Yogi-Avayogi, during the relevant MD-AD Periods and so on. Similarly, Indu Lagna signifies the source and blessings of wealth.

However, if one has the Pancha-Maha-Purusha yoga, wealth is imminent irrespective of the dignity of Indu Lagna in the chart.

'Karanam Karya Siddhim Cha' is the classical dictum. The essence of this dictum is – hold on to your Karana for all Success. Hence, I have attempted to deal with Karana in good detail based on my research. I have practically observed stunning outcomes upon worship of Karana Lord. For example, Garaja Karana resolves issues in getting a Progeny and Bhadra Karana in ensuring the good care of Parents.

The planets posited in yogi star, dole out a multiplier effect on even the ordinary yoga promised in the chart. On the other hand, there are natives who have lost their hard earned wealth due to their association with natives born in the star of Avayogi. If the Avayogi planet is placed in the 2nd Bhava, or if any planet in 2H is placed in Avayogi's star, it signifies a potential loss of wealth.

This book is intended not only for the Astrologers but also for all Astro-Enthusiasts in general. In fact, while covering these 4 broad topics, I felt so humbled by how it is a long unending journey of Astro-learning!!

I pray for the divine to bless us all to delve deeper into this divine knowledge with a better understanding and a wider perspective. I have published this book in my own style, and I trust this will benefit all the readers. My hearty greetings and blessings to you all.

With the abundant blessing of my lord Uchchhishta Maha Ganapathy, the Gurus and the Ancestors,

In service of divine astrology

– Tirupur S. Gopalakrishnan
9842220903
gkastro.tirupur@gmail.com

# FORWARD

## AUM GURAVE NAMAHA!!

At the outset, My Sadar Pranaams to My Master – GK Astro Sir, for giving this Bhagya to translate his writings & teachings on Thithi, Yoga & Karana and Indu Lagna. I am just one of Guruji's tens of thousands of Students – A Non descriptive one at that!

Astro GK Sir is a 24/7 Astro – Jyotish runs through His blood, Flesh & Veins – Very personification of What Jyotish is. Jyotish is a Tapas/ Yagna – for him, not a source of mere livelihood. He is a Tapaswi, A Colossus with no aspect of Jyotish uncovered or researched thus far.

His interpretations of several complex jyotish concepts like Retrograde, Parivartana and Yogas like Indu lagna, Rashmi yoga, Pancha mahapurusha and Naadi, Prashna etc. are unique with applied practical wisdom – derived from a massive data base of lac+ charts.

He has taught over 30000 students on various topics of Astrology & had recently established an "Astro Gurukul" to teach **'Astrology'** as a residential course for the students, who can't afford to pay fees

*He is a Living Legend – A Maharishi in the class of Sages of Yore without doubt.* He does not seek recognition nor into commercial ventures. But most Star Astrologers in Tamil Nadu – Respect him as a Genius & Legend. He is a Perennial source like River Ganga – Keeps flowing with Astrological dictums – always in abundance totally unfettered!!

## ABOUT THIS BOOK:

- ➢ This book is a translated version of Guruji's Original Tamil Version – Thithi, Karanam which included Yogi – Avayogi and Indu lagna too in addition. A brief note on the concept of MUDAKKU too is incorporated as a Bonus.
- ➢ We have incorporated a lot of additional Material from his teachings in class & various updated Q&A sessions with his students.
- ➢ We have attempted to present this in a Bullet point/ Numbered list module for easy comprehension and retention.
- ➢ Guruji is a repository of unlimited Vedic Astro wisdom & just shares his knowledge unhindered like a free flowing stream without blinking an eye lid. Trust we will be fortunate enough to come out with Additional Editions in the near future.
- ➢ There is not enough written material on Indu Lagna, Thithi, Yoga and Karana with their Predictive component (with example charts) available in the market. This is an attempt to address this shortage. Trust this book will a good tool-in-aid for predictions

*With Heart filled with Deep gratitude for His blessings bestowed upon this – a primitive soul in search of Jyoti!!*

Aum Gurave Namaha!!!

– Haraprasad R

# CHAPTER 1

# INDU LAGNA

---

A. **INDU LAGNA (IL)** – is the special Ascendant in the chart, signifying the wealth & prosperity, viz. the wealth & prosperity promised in this birth.

1. This indicates, the Net – Sum of the Bhagya/Luck of the native through a single consolidated source viz.if the wealth – prosperity as indicated in natal chart will multiply/ decrease. This also indicates different dimensions or sources of **Material Prosperity**.

2. After all, material wealth &prosperity – aka Dhana Yoga, is a very important and significant factor, to ensure a fairly comfortable life on this Mother Earth.

3. In fact, the very birth and livelihood, as a human being itself indicates possession of at least 30+ positive yogas in one's chart. One needs about 50+ Yogas (out of more than 100+ Yogas) to lead a decent quality of life.

4. Indu is Chandra (Moon) – but also signifies Indra – The king of Devas & therefore an indicator of Prosperity. Indu Lagna – is Chandra/Moon based & signifies wealth.

5. The planets Venus & Jupiter are the Significators of wealth & Moon gets exalted in Venus sign & Jupiter gets exalted in Moon's sign. Hence, the connection of Moon, to wealth is indispensable.

## B. Indu Lagna Calculation

1. Sage Parashara has mentioned this Dhana yoga as Moon Yoga. The wealth yoga is also dealt with by Sage Jaimini too, as Dhanapada.

2. Mahakavi Kalidasa has also elaborated on this Indu Lagna, in his Astro Epic – Uttra kalamitra. Each planet is assigned strength – in number, based on Kala-Rays they transmit upon this Earth.

3. This is transferred to the sign of their Lordships summarised as under:

| Table : The Rays/Kalas allotted for each planet & the Calculation of Indu Lagna(IL) | | | | | | |
|---|---|---|---|---|---|---|
| Planets | Sun | Moon | Venus | Jupiter | Mercury | Mars | Saturn |
| Kala/ Points | 30 | 16 | 12 | 10 | 8 | 6 | 1 |
| Remark | Apply these points to the signs lorded by these planets. Take the 9H from Lagna& moon. Add these two kalas/points – then divide by 12 – take the reminder. Count that no of houses from Moon- That is your Indu Lagna (IL).If the reminder is zero-then 12th house from Moon is the Indu Lagna | | | | | | |

4. The Sign wise rays are also represented in the Rashi chart as under

| 10 | 6 | 12 | 8 |
|---|---|---|---|
| 1 | Rays(Kalas) as per Rashis(Signs) | | 16 |
| 1 | | | 30 |
| 10 | 6 | 12 | 8 |

> ➤ It may be observed that there is a pattern in the Top & Bottom rows &that the Luminaries Moon & Sun are assigned the highest points (as they reflect more light on earth) & Saturn the farthest & darkest – the least one.

> ➤ The Author opines, as the base is Moon here-Indu Lagna may reflect the compounded Bhagya (Luck) of the native & mother. However, the exact calculation behind this assignment of values is known only to the Rishis (Though the total value sums up to 120-The Vimshottari Period)

5. Note:

Nineth Bhava (9H) signifies Luck & Bhagya. As Indu Lagna, essentially signifies Bhagya – The 9H from both Chandra & Lagna are taken – their Kalas (Rays) are added, which is then divided by 12 & the balance Number reflects the House, to be counted from Chandra-Moon. That's your Indu Lagna. If the reminder is zero-then 12th house from Moon is the Indu Lagna.

# Many Astro soft wares give this readily & can be referred to by the beginners.

## C. More on Indu Lagna

1. Initially there was no specific Lagna assigned for signifying wealth, before this concept of Indu Lagna came into practice. Also many researchers, dispute that this Indu Lagna – does not work & it's efficacy debatable.

2. However, unless one observes & identifies the circumstances under which this concept fails – there can't be any progress. The cases, where it works or fails to deliver, are dealt with in this book.

3. The Pancha Mahapurusha yogas & Dharma Karmathipathi Yoga are seminal yogas – that promise Stature & Fame. The Indu Lagna delivers its results, in sync with any of these 2 yogas. Most rich guys in this world, have this Indu Lagna, working in sync with the Pancha Mahapurusha yoga.

4. In general, if the Native has even one of the Major Pancha Mahapurusha yoga (PMPY) – He attains good heights. If the Indu Lagna too is, in good dignity along with this PMPY – he becomes very famous too. All these give good benefits, when they are in Kendra Bhava (Squares).

5. This in effect, reflects the sum total of Natives/Fathers/ Mothers Bhagya promised in the Chart.

## D. Example Charts for Calculation of Indu Lagna (IL).

**Chart-1**

| Moon 10 | 6 | Lagna 12 | 8 |
|---|---|---|---|
| 1 | Chart 1 Taurus Lagna with Moon in Pisces | | 16 |
| 1 | | | 30 |
| 10 | 6 | 12 | Indu Lagna 8 |

**Chart-2**

| 10 | Moon 6 | Lagna 12 | 8 |
|---|---|---|---|
| Indu Lagna1 | Chart 2 Taurus Lagna with Moon in Aries | | 16 |
| 1 | | | 30 |
| 10 | 6 | 12 | 8 |

**Chart-1:**

- The 9H from Lagna is Capricorn – Points is 1.
- The 9H from Moon is Scorpio – Points is 6
- Add these 2 points above =1+6=7.
- Hence the 7th sign from Moon is Virgo – is the Indu Lagna.

# as the total is less than 12-it was not divided by 12 & hence taken as it is.

#This Native has good prospects as the Indu Lagna is at 5th from Lagna &7th from Moon and hence IL is not afflicted.

**Chart-2**: Just replicate the above process – The Indu Lagna is at 11H from Moon

**Chart-3**

| 10 | 6 | 12 | 8 |
|---|---|---|---|
| Moon 1 | | | Indu Lagna 16 |
| 1 | | | 30 |
| Lagna 10 | 6 | 12 | 8 |

**Chart-4**

| 10 | Moon 6 | 12 | 8 |
|---|---|---|---|
| 1 | | | Indu Lagna 16 |
| 1 | | | 30 |
| Lagna 10 | 6 | 12 | 8 |

**Chart-3:**

> - The 9H from Lagna (SAG) is Leo – Points is 30.
> - The 9H from Moon (AQU) is Libra – Points is 12
> - Add these 2 points above =30+12=42.
> - Divide it by 12 – Reminder is 6
> - Hence the 6th sign from Moon is Cancer – is the Indu Lagna.

# As the total is more than 12-it is divided by 12 & the reminder is reckoned.

**Chart-4:** Just replicate the above process – The Indu Lagna is at 4H from Moon

## E. INDU LAGNA in PERSPECTIVE

1. Lagna (Ascendant) indicates the *Punya* of the Native. This Punya Lagna is inherited from the movement of SUN, which is the Karaka for father,

2. The 9th House from Lagna is the Bhagyasthan (Luck) – the Punya inherited by the Native. The 9th House from Moon is the Punya inherited by the Mother (Moon is the Mother).

3. Thus, the house of convergence of Natives Punya & the Mothers Punya in summation - is the House of Income-

Wealth, Dhana Bhagya of the Native. **This is the INDU LAGNA**

4. **Thus, the Indu Lagna is the point indicating the sum effect of Punya of the Native& Mother – transformed & reflected as a veritable Wealth Yoga.**

5. This also gets reflected as Yoga of fame in some cases – like **Late Kakkan** (An Ex Minister of TN) who accumulated no wealth but lasting fame. However, this comes after a struggle.

## F. Indu Lagna Yoga(s) – Few Snippets

1. **The Indu Lagna delivers its best results (150%) if it's posited in a Sthira – Rashi (Fixed sign).**

   ➢ Because fixed signs are stable & signify good retention of wealth.

   ➢ Thus if a Native gets married to a spouse with IL in a fixed sign-good wealth accumulation

   ➢ The Indu Lagna if, in a Chara Rashi (Movable sign), does not give full impact – only 75%.

   ➢ It delivers much less in a Dual Sign – Only 50%

**Thus Indu Lagna – if posited in a Fixed Sign delivers the best outcome – in wealth matters**

2. **There must be at least one planet in Indu Lagna-to deliver optimal results.**

   ➢ If there are no planets – the Native may not appreciate the value/feel its worth. Thus, it's better to have planet(s) in IL.

3. **If Indu Lagna is tenanted by an Exalted/Mool Trikona/ Swashetra/Dig Bala planet – Excellent(200%).**

   ➢ These need not be Benefics, but could be Malefics as well- Its just they need to be strong – like a skilled driver for a premium car.

4. **The Indu Lagna should not be in Dusthana – like in 6H-8H-12H from Lagna. The Native, does not get to enjoy the wealth even if endowed with**

5. **Multiple planets in Indu Lagna – also give good status-fame in addition to wealth. It's a potential Raja yoga**

6. **If the Indu Lagna has both, a Malefic & a Benefic planet(say Rahu+Jupiter) in conjunction – The native gets only 50% &the balance gets shared with his partner/others**

7. **If there are no planet(s) in Indu Lagna-if the Natal Lagna is posited with or aspected by a Benefic – Promises a good yoga to the native**

8. **Multiple Benefics in Indu Lagna – Dole out exponential benefits to the native-A sort of Vipareetha Rajayoga. If multiple Malefics, still a high wealth yoga, but probably, subject to other's scrutiny & criticism**

9. **Indu Lagna Lord if posited in IL itself – Immense benefit. If it's in Retrograde, delayed delivery but no denial**

10. **The profession signified by the planet in Indu Lagna or its Lord – are potential wealth creators**

11. **If the Lord of Indu Lagna (ILL) is afflicted, the Native is either deprived of the wealth yoga or unable to enjoy it even if in possession.**

> A planet is afflicted if it's close to Rahu or In Papa-kartari (hemmed between malefic)/debilitated/combust(astangada)

> Signs of Affliction

  ✓ Endowed with Power-Position but without responsibility – respect
  ✓ Priest without a temple attached
  ✓ Isolation even if endowed with multiple relatives, single/Separated from spouse

✓ In short, A pahalwan(Wrestler) without his core Strength-Power

## G. Rules

1. **In order to experience, enjoy the fruits of any Yoga, the Yogi planet should be connected either to the Lagna or the MD – AD-PAD Lords of the Native. If not, the Native will not get to enjoy the Yoga in full.**

   ➢ Ex: One Native seeks Prashna. He has 100 acres of land, but absolutely no cash on hand – even to purchase the seeds. Though endowed with property, is not enjoying it – because his Indu Lagna is afflicted

   ➢ **Thus it is important that the Yogi Planet is well placed & connected to the Lagna or Dasha lords(MD-AD-PAD)** in the prime periods of life, **in order to enjoy it's fruits**

2. **Avayogi in Indu Lagna**: The Native will resort to mindless spending; if he has cash on hand. Also will trouble his near & dear. It may prove to be counterproductive.

3. **Yogi in Indu Lagna**: The Native will keep multiplying his wealth& will not fritter away his gains. He will be balanced & matured in his approach

4. **Retrograde planet in Indu Lagna or ILL itself is a retrograde planet.**

   ➢ The Native will tend to wait or procrastinate to optimise the gains – Yogam, but without success

   ➢ Ex: The seller may hold his stock – so that he can sell it at a higher price, but then the market may crash. Students may wait & make another attempt to score higher marks in competitive exams like JEE/NEET, but without success

5. **If the Indu Lagna lord is a Natural benefic** (Ju, Ve, Mer, Moon (SP), the source of wealth will be a respectable one – say from father etc.

6. **If the Indu Lagna lord is a Malefic** (Sat, Mars, Sun, Moon(KP),

   ➢ The wealth may not be from respectable sources or means
   ➢ By wrongful acts, exploitation, doubtful means & sources like Liquor sales etc.
   ➢ However, if this Malefic is in strength, It may turn a Shubha – benefic & shall be useful for his family's progress

7. **If a Benefic & Malefic closely conjunct (say within 3°) in Indu Lagna :**

   ➢ The fruits of wealth will not be useful to the native – it gets enjoyed by the relationship signified by that Bhava like 5H – children etc.

   Example

| | | | |
|---|---|---|---|
| Saturn<br>Rahu Venus<br>Indu lagna | Example<br>Chart | | |
| | | | Ketu |
| | | Lagna | |

   ➢ Lagna – Libra, Indu Lagna in Aquarius-5th from Lagna. The Planets Saturn& Venus in 5H – Aquarius, which is a close conjunction, of a Natural benefic and malefic.
   ➢ **This implies that the Native will not get the wealth benefits during his prime time – but during his children's hey days – The Native however suffers still.**

## 8. Indu lagna lord in Parivartana

> Such Natives should keep transferring their gains – properties in their close confidant's name. Then only they can retain the fruits & enjoy

> If anybody gets into partnership with any Native having Indu Lagna lord in Parivartana – as a business partner, that guy will certainly break the partnership & leave in the middle

Example

| | | | |
|---|---|---|---|
| Indu lagna | Example Chart | | |
| Venus | | | |
| | | Saturn | |

> Lagna Aquarius which also doubles up as Indu Lagna too. The Landlord(LL) Saturn is in Parivartana with Venus
> This Native entered into a partnership business with his longtime friend – but parted ways soon.
> They had to split their holdings & also parted ways permanently
> **Hence such Natives with ILL in Parivartana should keep transferring their assets in their close confidant's name – for retention. This also applies, even if the Lagna lord is in Parivartana.**
> They should also be careful in giving up power, to the others like POA – else very difficult to get back.

## 9. The Planets posited in 6, 8, 12(Dusthana) from Indu Lagna

> During the MD-AD-PAD periods of the planets in Dustana from Indu Lagna – The benefits doled out by Indu Lagna gets reversed

- ➤ If it's the planets in 12H from Indu Lagna, the planet which gave the benefit takes it back
- ➤ Any planet promising Yoga – if placed in a Dusthana – gets the benefit returned back.

**Example chart-1**

| Lagna, Venus Jupiter | | | | | Lagna Venus, Jupiter | Indu Lagna | | |
|---|---|---|---|---|---|---|---|---|
| Indu Lagna | Native Saved Money 17/01/1998 | | | | | Native lost Money 17/01/1998 | | |
| | | | | | | | | |
| | | | | | | | | |

- ➤ This implies that if the Dhana karakas are in Lagna & posited in a favorable Bhava to the Indu Lagna – here 2H, it doles out high wealth
- ➤ If the Lagna & Wealth karakas are in Dustana, say in 12H from Indu Lagna, it indicates loss of wealth

## 10. Indu Lagna in Thithi Shunya Rashi

- ➤ This is a most undesirable placement. Whenever the Native gets wealth – it inflicts some deficiency/defect to the native or someone in the family viz. The native may be a rich man, but got a physically challenged child etc.
- ➤ Ex : Case of a Native with Indu Lagna in Thithi Shunya

This Native got into a major car accident & got a hefty compensation from the car company. He starts a textile shop with that money, which grows into a big enterprise soon

➢ But he is confined to a wheel chair – commands care & respect because he wields the financial power.

➢ Because it's in Thithi Shunya, he must be careful that he does not cede his power to others – if he does, he may lose his wealth & care.

➢ Ex: One such native with IL & ILL in Thithi Shunya gets married to a female, to better his financial prospects. His spouse goes back to her parents' house after a dispute – never returned. His properties too got locked with her.

**# Indu Lagna should not be with the lord of the Thithi Shunya Rashi (Daghda/Zero sign) as its more cruel**
**Example 2**

| Indu Lagna Jupiter * | | | |
|---|---|---|---|
| | *Dwitiya–SAG/PIS are in TS | | |
| | | | |
| * | | | Lagna |

➢ Lagna Virgo, Indu Lagna – Pisces with ILL Jupiter too in Pieces. He is born in Dwitiya Thithi – for which Sagittarius & Pisces are Thithi Shunya Rashis (Daghda Rashis).

➢ Hence IL & ILL both in Thithi Shunya, Daghda, a virulent combination.

➢ This Native was in great debt & hence marries a rich lady for her wealth. However, the lady leaves him after a fight & his efforts for reconciliation failed. His intent to get relief from his financial misery came a cropper & his reputation too got a beating. – This is the effect of IL & ILL – both in Thithi Shunya.

***Thus, The Indu Lagna in Thithi Shunya, along with its lord is double trouble**

## 11. Indu Lagna & Physical Deficiency

Example: 3

| | Lagna Ketu | | Indu lagna |
|---|---|---|---|
| Saturn | | | |
| | 07-12-1994 | | |
| Moon | Salem(TN) | | Mars |
| | Jupiter Sun Mercury | Venus Rahu | |

- ➤ Lagna Aries & Indu Lagna – Gemini with its lord Mercury in 6H from Indu Lagna & 8H from Lagna.
- ➤ This Native has physical challenges – got a govt job under this quota, yet could not hold onto it.

## 12. Query: Business, Self-employment & Indu Lagna.

- ➤ In general if Moon is posited in 4-6-8-12, Business – Self-employment should not be resorted to, if it involves Heavy investment (Consultancy is ok) – possible losses, failures.
- ➤ Similarly if the Indu lagna is at 2-5-9$^{th}$ from Lagna – such natives should not create or commence a new business. However, they can administer or run a business started/ created by somebody else. ( 9H is Administration)
- ➤ If they align their profession wrt. The Significations of the planet in Indu Lagna, Profit guaranteed.
- ➤ However prior to this, the above conditions for Business – Self-employment needs to be checked

## Example: 4

| | | | Moon |
|---|---|---|---|
| Saturn<br>Indu Lagna<br><br>Lagna | | 17-01-1998 | |
| | | | |

The Moon is at 6H from Lagna Capricorn & is the 7L too. The LL Saturn is in the Indu Lagna of Aquarius – 2H & in Mool Trikona.

> ➢ This Native tried his hands at several businesses – but failed.
> ➢ However, he was very successful whenever he administered the business of others.
> ➢ This LL-ILL Saturn while supporting success while working for others – failed him when he tried to be on his own

## Example: 5

| Lagna | Mercury<br>Indu Lagna | | |
|---|---|---|---|
| | | 17-01-1998 | |
| | | Moon | |

> ➢ Lagna – Pisces, Moon in 8H – Libra and Indu Lagna is in Aries with Mercury.
> ➢ The Native is an Astrologer, not highly educated was employed in a pvt firm.
> ➢ This Native has become famous by just learning the basics in astrology & daily predictions. He charges a hefty amount in suggesting Names to organisations.

- ➤ He is a good orator & attractive speaker – The karaka for speech, Mercury is posited in Indu Lagna & hence earns a lot. He has regular income & is popular – through his good speech, irrespective of if, the organisations-consulted are doing well or not. This is the power of Indu Lagna.

**Example: 6**

|  | Lagna Moon |  |  |
|---|---|---|---|
|  | 25-12-1982 |  |  |
|  | Indu Lagna Jupiter | Saturn |  |

- ➤ Aries Lagna with Moon in Lagna. Saturn in 7H – Libra & in Digbala. Indu Lagna is in Scorpio 8H with Jupiter therein.
- ➤ The planet in Indu Lagna is Jupiter – The karaka for teacher & children. Hence he gained in status after becoming a Teacher & grew wealthy after getting children
- ➤ **# If one resorts to the profession signified by the planet in Indu Lagna – it activates the wealth yoga.**
- ➤ He joins the school & administers it too. Then, he leaves the school – because they paid less, but was recalled & reinstated with a higher salary offer.
- ➤ The school grew multifold in strength (from 100 to 1800 students) under his administration. The 10-11th Lord Saturn exalted & in Digbala supports him along with ILL & the planet in Indu Lagna
- ➤ Saturn indicates Service – Seva & he precisely does that – in sync with the Indu Lagna planet – Jupiter signified profession.

## Example: 7

| Venus | | | |
|---|---|---|---|
| | | | |
| | | | |
| | | Indu Lagna | |

> Libra is the Indu Lagna with its lord Venus Exalted in Pisces – He is the one of the Richest man in the world

## Example:8

| Jupiter<br>Indu Lagna | | | |
|---|---|---|---|
| | | | |
| | | | |
| | | | |

> Pisces is the Indu Lagna with its Lord Jupiter too in IL.
> This Native rose to become the CM of a state from a big party – in a very short time during his Jupiter AD

## Example: 9

| Indu Lagna<br>Venus | | Lagna | |
|---|---|---|---|
| | | | |
| | | | |
| | Moon<br>Jupiter | Saturn | |

- Taurus Lagna, Moon in 7H of Scorpio with Jupiter & the Indu Lagna is Pisces with LL Venus exalted.
- This Native created a record of sorts in Industry & contributed to the development of high industrial growth in India & high status in society.
- This happened in his Venus AD period.
- His Moon is in debility & yet he succeeded. It's because – it is in 7H & not in Dusthana 6-8-12 which signifies possible failures – even if in exaltation.
- Moon, even if in debility, but posited in the Kendra houses of 1-7-10 signifies good dignity
- Note: Shri.Kamaraj, Shri.Annadurai, Shri.Karunanidhi – Ex CMs of Tamilnadu & Ex PM – Jawaharlal Nehru – **all had no planets in Indu Lagna – yet attained fame & name.**
- But they all had – Pancha Mahapurusha Yoga (PMPY) in good dignity. Natives with PMPY attain great power & fame.
- **# If PMPY is there in the chart – there is no need for existence of Indu Lagna Yoga.**
- PMPY is the highest yoga, can take the Natives to great heights on their own strength, irrespective of the delivery of the wealth yoga like Indu Lagna!
- Note: Those having one of their parents or ancestors – who were Tapaswis with good spiritual progress by controlling their Pancha-indriyas (5 senses), will be born with these PMPY in their life

## Example:10

| Jupiter, Lagna | | | |
|---|---|---|---|
| Moon | | | Indu Lagna |
| | | | |
| | | | |

- ➤ In general Moon in 12H does not support business. This Native was unemployed & was dependent on his parents. Yet, got married & then got a child too.
- ➤ Then joins a company as an advisor & consultant, expands his reach by becoming consultant to many firms, starts his own consultation Firm & becomes rich
- ➤ This Native is born in Lagna Pisces with its lord Jupiter therein &Moon in Aquarius. Hence his Indu Lagna is Cancer, which is aspected by Jupiter from Pisces.
- ➤ If there are no planets in Indu lagna – the wealth yoga gets activated, once the Native begets the relationship signified by the planet aspecting the Indu Lagna.
- ➤ Here he got good wealth after the birth of his children – which all happened during Jupiter MD, AD sub periods
- ➤ **Rule: If there are no planets in Indu Lagna – but if it receives aspects from a Benefic planet in strength, gives good benefits**

**Example:11**

| | | | |
|---|---|---|---|
| | | | |
| | | | Indu Lagna |
| Jupiter | | | |

- ➢ Indu lagna is in Leo, which is aspected by Jupiter (in Uttrashada) from Sagittarius – A first rate wealth yoga.
- ➢ This Jupiter's 9th aspect is highly beneficial, because Jupiter is a first rate Benefic for Leo
- ➢ Jupiter in his own & Mool Trikona house
- ➢ Lastly it's aspecting the Indu Lagna lord from LL's star of Uttrashada
- ➢ He is a wealthy & Prosperous businessman

**Example: 12**

| | | Indu Lagna | | | | Indu Lagna |
|---|---|---|---|---|---|---|
| | Jupiter in Moon's Star | | | | Jupiter in Sun's Star | |
| Jupiter | | | | Jupiter | | |
| | | | | | | |

- ➢ Check both the charts. The Indu Lagna is in Cancer & Jupiter is in Capricorn aspecting Indu Lagna.
- ➢ In the first chart – Jupiter is placed in the Star S'ravana, of ILL – Moon & aspects the Indu Lagna, which is an excellent proposition

- ➢ In the second one – Jupiter aspects the Indu Lagna from the Star of Sun (Uttrashada) & Sun has no connection with Indu Lagna – Not high wealth yoga.
- ➢ **The Rule is, the Indu Lagna, if receives aspects from a Benefic – Planet posited in its own** Lord's **star, is a first rate wealth yoga.**
  - ✓ Here, even if Jupiter is in debility, because it's posited in the Star of ILL & casts its aspect on Indu Lagna – it's bound to give high wealth. **Mere Benefic aspect on Indu Lagna – is not a sufficient condition for delivery of wealth**

## 13. Indu Lagna & Gochara (Transits)

- ➢ The Natural Wealth Karaka planets – Jupiter & Venus, whenever they transit over the Indu Lagna – dole out wealth. Thus every Native will receive some gains – Every year & once in 12 years respectively.
- ➢ **The gains are optimal – if these Shubha Planets aspect the Indu Lagna from the Star of the ILL (Indu Lagna lord)**
- ➢ The timing of the gains of wealth – are decided by the Dasha – Bukti & Gochara of these concerned planets. The MD-AD of planets in Indu Lagna or the planets aspecting the Indu Lagna are pivotal.
- ➢ **No yoga gets delivered without the positive concurrence of Dasha – Bukti & Gochara.**
- ➢ The promise of Wealth yoga is indicated in the Natal chart – However, its deliverance is signified/realized only by Dasha – Bukti & Gochara.

## Example: 13 (Female Native)

| | | | | | | |
|---|---|---|---|---|---|---|
| Lagna | | Indu Lagna | | | Gochara | |
| Venus | Natal | | | Saturn Jupiter Venus | | |
| | | | | | | |

- ➤ Female Native, Aquarius Lagna with Indu Lagna in Cancer. Venus in Capricorn – 7$^{th}$ from Indu Lagna
- ➤ The sign Capricorn is being transited over by Venus, Jupiter & Saturn
- ➤ Here the Indu Lagna is at 6H from Lagna & hence this Native started a Mill by taking a bank loan – she is the first generation entrepreneur. Most of her profits go towards loan repayment.
- ➤ However, she still takes 25k as income from business as against the paltry 5K; she used to receive as a temporary employee. This fructified, when Jupiter transited over Natal Venus in Gochara.
- ➤ This position gives some steady & lasting wealth
- ➤ Note: Good gains – only when the Dhana karakas Jupiter & Venus transit over/aspect Indu Lagna or during their MD – AD periods. **No Yoga/incident fructifies without the involvement of Gochara & Dasha – Bukti.**

## Example: 14

| Indu Lagna | | | |
|---|---|---|---|
| | | | |
| | | | |
| | Moon | Jupiter | |

- ➢ Taurus Lagna Native with Indu Lagna in Pisces, with its lord Jupiter at Libra& Moon in Scorpio.
- ➢ The Indu Lagna lord Jupiter is 8th from Indu Lagna, 6th from Lagna & 12th from Moon. Hence in Dusthana, from all the 3 important Lagnas.
- ➢ He started a business in his Jupiter AD – which initially looked very promising, but after certain sudden events – incurred heavy losses – 40 lacs plus & is out of business
- ➢ Here the Indu Lagna lord is connected to the Natal Lagna or LL & is also at a Dusthana from Indu Lagna. Hence, though had a promising start – was unable to retain & sustain his gains.

**Thus, the Indu Lagna lord if in Dustana 6-8-12 does not support retention or sustenance of the benefits of the Wealth Promised.**

## Example: 15

| | | Indu Lagna Moon Venus | |
|---|---|---|---|
| Sun Mars | | | |
| | Male Native | | |
| | | | |

- ➤ Indu lagna is in Taurus, with the Indu Lagna lord Venus & Moon (Exalted & in Mool Trikona) posited there. Also Sun & Mars (Digbala) in 10th from Indu Lagna.
- ➤ This Native started off as a labourer, grew into a great film financier & rich. Also runs an idly shoppe, because Indu lagna has Moon (signifies food).
- ➤ He looks very simple and with 4 planets in good dignity amassed wealth in their MD – AD periods.
- ➤ **The Indu Lagna has 2 Benefics, the wealth yoga, played out after he got married (Venus is kalatra karaka).This wealth yoga, got transformed into a Raja yoga with 2 planets in Kendra Bhava – 10H & in Digbala.**

14. **In short, the PMPY (Pancha Maha Purusha) yoga gives fame, status & wealth, whereas Indu Lagna just signifies wealth – that too less than PMPY.**

- ➤ Indu lagna delivers the wealth yoga if tenanted by Benefics. If tenanted by Malefics, they should be in good dignity like in Swashetra, Mool Trikona or Uccha-Exaltation!

15. **The Author's Take:**

- ✓ Indu lagna results are prominent & visible – if the Natal chart is an average one.
- ✓ For the Natives with good Pancha Maha Purusha Yoga (PMPY) and/or Dharma Karmathipathi Yoga (DKAY), the effect of Indu Lagna is not felt prominently.

16. **Indu Lagna Wealth Yoga Rule – 1**

**If the Indu Lagna is not in Dusthana to the Natal Lagna with Jupiter& Moon posited** there **– either in conjunction or in Trine – Signifies a good Wealth yoga.**

**Example: 16**

|  | Indu Lagna |  | Lagna |
|---|---|---|---|
| Sun |  |  |  |
|  |  |  | Moon |
| Jupiter |  |  |  |

|  |  | Jupiter |  |
|---|---|---|---|
|  |  |  | Lagna |
| Moon |  |  |  |
|  | Sun Mercury |  | Indu Lagna |

> ➢ It can be observed here that the Indu Lagna is not in 6/8/12 to the Natal Lagna. Both Jupiter & Moon are posited in trine to the Indu Lagna. Hence signifies a veritable Wealth yoga.

> ➢ The late PM Smt Indira Gandhi & CM Ms.Jayalalitha had these & enjoyed a good Dhana (wealth) yoga

## 17. Indu Lagna Wealth Yoga Rule – 2: If Rahu is posited in Indu Lagna

> ➢ It drives the Native to amass wealth through short cuts & not so fair means – Such people land up in avoidable problems too, as a consequence, mostly.

> ➢ **The Rule is – The Native aspires to multiply/grow his wealth in accordance with the signification (Karakatwa) of the planet posited in Indu Lagna.**

## 18. The right Muhurta to start or execute a plan to make money:

> ➢ **When the Gochara Lagna transits over your Indu Lagna or Its Lord (ILL).However, Avoid the Muhurta – when the Indu Lagna lord is weak in Gochara like in combustion, debility etc.**

- ➤ This can be tested with observing the days – in which one earns the least and the most, in relation to the status of Indu lagna

- ➤ A Native with position in power – suddenly comes & insists that his case should be predicted on priority & he can pay premium fees. Then it turned out that he meant the horoscopes of his entire family – not his alone.

- ➤ This showed that his Indu Lagna lord was Combust in Transit at that time

- ➤ Likewise, any planning for a new wealth creating activity – should be done when the Indu Lagna lord is in strength in Gochara & in consultation with others

- ➤ **Thus, even if the Indu Lagna lord is weak in the Natal chart, Any development plan or Activity should be carried out only when the ILL is in good dignity – strength in Gochara – Transit**

## 19. INDU Alias PURNIMA MOON

- ➤ INDU is Chandra – Moon. Moon is at its best & complete at the time of Purnima – when it is exactly at 180° to the Sun.

- ➤ The period of 16 minutes prior & after this Full Purnima (Total 32 minutes) is called Shodasi – Lorded by the Davata Shodasi.

- ➤ This is most ideal time to pray – penance to minimise the ill or negative effect of Indu Lagna & also helps to better the wealth prospects.

- ➤ Those who are well versed in this Mantra Japa – should commence this process 24 minutes before Purnima & until 24 minutes afterwards. (Total – 48 minutes). Otherwise 16 minutes earlier.

- ➤ If there are more planets in Indu Lagna, this process should be continued for 56 weeks to get optimal outcome.

20. **Lastly – Even though the Indu Lagna lord** promises **wealth yoga – its actual delivery is primarily during its concerned MD – AD – PAD periods** only **– not in other periods.**

## H. Few Additional Pointers & Summary in Brief

1. The Primary wealth indicators are 2H, 11H & their lords. If the Indu Lagna falls in 2H/11H – it's a multiplier of wealth. Also strong planets in 2H&11H to Indu Lagna, promise immense wealth. Thus the Indu Lagna, indicates more wealth than what is promised, but with less effort

2. The Natural Benefics like Jupiter/Venus/Wax. Moon/Mercury, if placed in Indu Lagna, promise good wealth & prosperity

3. Exalted Malefics & Malefics with Benefic aspects also give good wealth.

4. If this Lagna is tenanted by an Exalted/Mool Trikona/ Swashetra/Dig Bala planet – Excellent

5. If there are more than 1 planet in IL, the concurrent MD/AD/ PAD of the planets conjunct – is very positive

6. If there are No planets – The Lord of Indu Lagna (ILL) gives benefit – but to the extent of 50%

7. If there are multiple planets – The planet with the Highest Degree(HD) will have the Power, authority to give the benefits, followed by others in far lesser proportion

8. Malefic & weak Benefic like Combusted, Retrograde, Debilitated & Planets in Thithi Shunya Rashi – fail to give results in Indu Lagna

   ➢ Remedy: When you earn – invest/save it in somebody else's name (Deposit/Gold/Property).

   ➢ If Benefic – it will find a way to resort to this above mentioned solution

> If Malefic – Requires External Aid, Consultancy, say from an Astrologer, Investment expert etc.
> If it's in TS – The wealth will come but will disappear soon. Hence the remedy

9. In Muhurta for a Job/Business – If they commence the work in the Nakshatra of the Indu Lagna planet (ILL) – Easy success.

10. **Thus, IL has the influence to convert an ordinary Dhanyoga into a** Mahayoga of **multiple proportions.**

11. Indu Lagna's placement – Bhava indicates the source of wealth.

> Ex: IL is in 12H – Wealth & Prosperity if moved to foreign/ Native place. IL is in 5H – Prosperity after Child birth – through creativity etc.
> IL is in 7H – Through Spouse & Partners
> IL falls in the 10H from Natal Lagna – It Indicates – that the Native will respect & value the Wealth generated by his own efforts & not through inheritance – Gifts. Thus this also gives – Prestige & Self Esteem in the matter of wealth

> # Thus, **the sum of wealth signified by 2H/11H & its lords in a chart, is single handily given by IL**

12. Planets in Indu Lagna:

> Jupiter (JU) in IL: Prosperity after child birth, Growth through JU signified professions like Teacher, Mentor etc.
> This fructifies during its MD/AD/PAD & favourable transit of JU over this & it's star
> Ex: Sun in IL for Leo Moon Sign Native. He rose to a very high level only in politics – though he attempted different professions before.

13. If you want to sustain prosperity/Wealth, marry a Girl with her Indu Lagna (IL)/ILL in a Sthira Rashi – Fixed sign (2/5/8/11 H of KPC)

14. Retrograde (Vakri) Planet in IL: You will not get the desired results – Keeps Waiting or Delayed outcome.

15. Shubha Graha (Benefic) in IL or as Lord of IL: Will get wealth with respect & respectable means

16. Papa Graha (Malefic) in IL or as Lord of IL: Will get wealth – but not through a not so respectable source – say through a liquor shop sales etc.

17. Parivartana of IL: They go out Empty handed

   ➢ Ex: One Business man with a high investment business with 2 partners. It was doing well, but got evicted by other two using a mischievous clause in its bye – law

18. Indu Lagna in Thithi Shunya: It gives wealth but with a defect/deficiency!

   ➢ Ex: A guy got into an Accident & got heavy compensation. But lost his limbs – unable to enjoy
   ➢ A young Girl – May get wealth by marrying a Rich old Man – But no Marital charm etc.

19. Tithi Shunya lord in Indu Lagna. If TSL in IL: Adverse after effects – separation after Marriage – disappointment/feeling cheated etc.

20. Difference between Indu Lagna (IL)/ILL & Normal Wealth Significators (2H-11H/2L-11L):

   ➢ The Former (IL-ILL) is Wealth through Punya/Luck
   ➢ The Later (2-11) wealth through Own Efforts

21. The Worship time for Indu Lagna is – when the moon is at its brightest – darkest. it's before & after 16 minutes of Purnima & Amavasya

   Pray that all members are blessed by Indra & Chandra in Abundance

# CHAPTER 2

# KARANA

───◦◦◦───

"AUM GAM GANAPATHAYE NAMAHA"

"AUM GURAVE NAMAHA"

## A. PANCHANGA:

1. **Panchanga is a Primordial Element of Vedic Astrology.** No Vedic astrological chart is complete without the details of Panchanga, which essentially signifies the effects of interaction between the SUN & MOON through its five limbs viz...

   i.   **Fire** Through **Vaara** (weekday/Solar day)
   ii.  **Earth** Through **Thithi**
   iii. **Air** Through **Karana***
   iv.  **Water** Through **Nakshatra**
   v.   **Akash** Through **Yoga**

   (*Note: The classification of TATVA Elements for Each Limb of Panchanga is not specific in Classical texts. The above classification of Panchanga Elements under the 5 Tatvas is based on their working in Medical Astrology as classified by the author. This varies like *Karana is Earth or Akash as per few Other Traditions. Definitions of other elements too differ. Our Focus here is more on the Applied Aspects of **Karana**.)

2. Every human being is made up of these five elements, aka Pancha-bhutas. Such a continuous interaction between the Sun & Moon causes dynamic transformation of energies, which affect every human being, in a unique way. This finds its use in medical astrology as well.

3. Understanding its impact, in relation to the individual birth chart is a fascinating subject for any Jyotish. After all, jyotish is a study of such a light, with the luminaries' sun & moon as the fulcrum.

   **#Note:** *The Karana lordships/Devata does vary as per the traditions in Kerala, Tamilnadu & North and not much of classical references are readily available in print for authentication.*

4. This book will essentially focus on the impact of **Karana** on human life particularly with reference to one's Vedic birth chart as researched and experienced by the Original **Author – GK Astro Sir.** The impact on **Muhurta** too is factored therein.

## B. KARANA in Brief:

1. A Karana (6°) is just half of a Tithi (12°). It is essentially the time taken in steps, when the angular distance between Sun and Moon increases by 6° starting from 0°.The Sun & Moon are conjunct on Amavasya and exactly opposite on Purnima at 180°. Accordingly, there are 30 Karana(s) during the Waxing phase (0°-180°) & another 30 Karana(s) during the waning phase of the Moon (181° – 0°). Thus, there are 60 Karana(s) covering one Monthly cycle of 360°.

2. However, there are only 11 Karana's defined in Vedic Astrology in total. Out of which 7 are considered as Movable (Chara Karana) and the remaining 4 as Fixed (Sthira Karana).

3. The Seven **Chara Karanas**, get repeated 8 times in a month (8*7 =56) from No.2 to No.57 as sequenced hereunder:

   i. Bava (2,9,16,23,30,37,44,51)
  ii. Balava (3,10.17.24.31,38,45,52)
 iii. Kaulava (4,11,18,25,32,39,46,53)
  iv. Taitula (5,12,19,26,33,40,47,54)
   v. Garaja(Gar) (6,13,20,27,34,42,48,55)
  vi. Vanija (7,14,21,28,35,42,49,56)
 vii. Bhadra – Vishti (8,15,22,29,36,43,57)

The Four **Fixed (Sthira) Karana** are

   i. Shakuni (58)
  ii. Chatushpada(59)
 iii. Naga (60)
  iv. Kinstughna (1)

4. The first 7 Karana's are known as 'Chara', which means 'Variable' and the last 4 Karana's are called as 'Sthira' which means 'Constant'.

   ➢ First 7 Karana are known as Chara, because they come repeatedly, in a specific sequence, covering the period starting from the second half of Shukla Paksha (Bright Fortnight) Pratipda and ending with first half of Krishna Paksha (Dark Fortnight) Chaturdashi. They are all considered auspicious (98%) except Bhadra (Vishti).

   ➢ Last 4 are known as 'Sthira' because, they always come during a specific period starting from the second half of Krishna Paksha (Dark Fortnight) Chaturdashi and ending with first half of Shukla Paksha (Bright Fortnight) Pratipada.

5. They are mostly inauspicious (90%), as they don't get the light of the luminary Moon. Hence Muhurta for relationships are avoided in Sthira Karana.

6. Actual Occurrence of each Karana in the specific sequence, is indicated in parenthesis (), against each Karana as above.

## C. KARANA & KARANA LORD

1. **The word "KARANA" implies activity. It sprouts from "Kru", which is the Dhatu root word "to do".** The Karana, not only represents the Karmic (Action) effects inherited from the past action, but also the current possibilities and their cause & effect. It defines the work we do & the areas of work/ profession where we can excel. It implies **KARYA SIDDHI.**

2. **Thithi** is all about desires & relationships and **Karana** is all about the **Karma/Action,** we perform on this mother earth to achieve or realize those desires. Check 'Thithi Shunya' for identifying such desires. **Karana** helps in annihilation of **Thithi**

**Shunya** blockages. Also Karana activates the **Fortuna point** in many cases.

3. The **Karana lord (KL)**, not only signifies the skills we are good at, but also helps to identify our mistakes & possible course correction, to enable its optimal dispensation. After all, the Purpose of each soul is to shed the entire karmic load & become one with the Divine. **Karana lord (KL)** helps in attainment of **Karya siddhi/Karma phal**

4. #Karana Gandanta, point of transit to the ensuing Karana viz. Karana at 0° implies a major defect in the Native

5. Each Karana owes its lordship to a particular planet-Graha in the solar system & which is designated as the **Karana Lord – KL**

6. The **KL** has a primary responsibility to ensure the fruits of one's action viz... **Karya Siddhi/Karma Phal** is in accordance with its mandated significations. The **KL** also reflects our inherent potential, to perform a work & create wealth.

7. The **KL**, if posited alone in the natal chart, mostly helps in the career/work and profession associated with its own significations. If, in association with any other planet by PAC, helps through the associated planet's significations as well.

8. Karana also implies **Vasana-smell/Swaas**. There is a saying in Tamil "Karanam Thappinal Maranam" – No life if Karana is missed.

9. Karana activates the Fortuna-point also. Fortuna point is arrived at by adding the lagna degree with Thithi degree. If the Fortuna point is within 7°from lagna, it's Shukla Paksha. If it's between 8°-12°from lagna – it's Krishna Paksha.

10. The natives born in one of these 11 Karana's will reflect the concerned animal/birds characters and activities, including their orientation in sexual acts as well.

## D. All these 11 Karana(s) are dealt with in detail as under:

## 1. BAVA

### I. General Characteristics

a. This Karana is very auspicious & the natives, very spiritual. But they have more faith in hard work/duty than bakthi.

b. This Karana occurs near Purnima & never in the vicinity of Amavasya. Hence it's natives always have a bright disposition & royalty

c. This Karana is symbolized by a Lion and Leadership. They have soft-nice hair too.

d. The BAVA Karana Natives
   If have more planets in Male Rashis –
   - ✓ Lazy & Bulky, Impatient & not respectful
   - ✓ But Target & Result oriented – Highly successful

   If have more planets in Female Rashis:
   - ✓ Active & Energetic, Light
   - ✓ High Patience & Respectful
   - ✓ Lack focus & hence less efficient
   - ✓ *Females are more active but need Male support for completion

e. The Lion roars before commencing the fight (direct & open challenge – very Dharmic)

f. They mostly possess own shelters but are contented in attitude.

g. They provide inheritance to progeny (Wealth)

h. Sustain a desire for frequent copulation

i. Native & Spouse – both in employment

j. They should not marry a soft person, whose Karana reflects a soft animal. Else, it inflicts hormonal issues

k.  A retro Mars in natal chart ensures success in legal battle. Bava Karana adds its support to such a success without losses & expenses

l.  They are highly status conscious/love comforts. Even if born in a nominal background are broadminded, liberal & highly ethical

m.  Very courageous, get lot of appreciation/rewards in competitions. They desire celebrations, fond of gifts & prizes

n.  They eat less & spend less for themselves, but spend a lot for others/sycophants

o.  Hence, it's better for them to hold their assets jointly, rather than individually

p.  They are protective of their spouse (Don't stare at their spouse)

q.  They love Jyotish-Astrology and good in research

r.  They are showmen and also unique in their execution of any work

s.  Good for professions requiring Leadership – Admin & Management, Army, Police, Civil Service.

t.  Possess Mercurial-character. They may have to be monitored by others even for sleeping and getting up

u.  If not Hungry for long, need to check for diseases. They don't waste food.

v.  They are fairly balanced & peaceful. Good support from Government.

w.  This symbolizes productive organs. They may have more iron/calcium in their body.

x.  They don't look back once on a mission.

y.  Likely problems for Bhava Karana natives-They may be jobless in some cases

## II. **Muhurta:**

a. Very auspicious esp. during the first half (5.5 Hours) of Bava

b. Good for success in competitions

c. Good for participating in Auctions

d. Good for consultancy & finalisation of contracts

e. Wedding Muhurta in Bava Karana – harmonious conjugal Life

f. Ex: Removes Sarpa dosha etc. in Horoscope.

## III. **Remedies & Suggestions**

a. Good to Keep Lion picture/Screen savers – but Keep changing them after every achievement of success

b. Worship: Surya Namaskar during sunrise to mitigate any negativity. Also, Shiva worship.

c. Worship of Simha Vahini/Durga for solution to problems/ Upasana

d. The Pooja Samagri/Davata is tabulated as under. The Natives are advised to make use of these items & worship with Dhoop/Deepa/Naivedhya after Archana & Alankar for optimal results.

## IV. Worship Details

| Table 1 | | | | | |
|---|---|---|---|---|---|
| **Bhava Karana – Devata's and other associated items for remedy & worship** | | | | | |
| SL No | Description | Associated Deities/Items | SL No | Description | Associated Deities/Items |
| 1 | Ruling Planet | Mars/*Sun | 8 | Paste/ Powder | Kasturi Manjal (Wild Turmeric) |
| 2 | Vara | Tuesday/ *Sunday | 9 | Cloth (Vastram) | White Cloth |
| 3 | Athi Davata | Lord Indra/ Devendra | 10 | Gemstone | Ruby |
| 4 | Deities | Narasimha, Hanuman (Standing) Simha Vahini, Aditya | 11 | Dhoop | Akil Kattai/ Aloe Wood |
| 5 | Animal | Lion | 12 | Metal/Vessel | Gold |
| 6 | Dhanya-Cereal | Arhar/Toor Dhal Red Gram | 13 | Flower | Punnai Malar/ Alexandrian Laurel Flower |
| 7 | Food/ Naivedhya | Anna Dhan (Rice-Chaval) Sweet Pongal | 14 | Idol/Portrait | Simha Vahini |

*Other traditions

## V. Additional Pointers

a. Grow & Worship Punnai Tree (Alexandrian Laurel) & flowers for Puja

b. Annadhan-Donate Meals, after worship of Karana Lord

c. Females can use Wild turmeric for bath & Males can gift this for temples.

d. One lady was advised to use this daily & this helped her unite with her deserted spouse.

e. Similarly another native used this turmeric with Kunkum as Bindhi & got her problems with bosses resolved. Likewise use white cloths, Doop, Prasad as suggested above for good outcomes

f. One Native in BAVA (Lazy guy) got married in this Karana, but remained jobless for 16 years. Such sudden job losses are possible. They may need their family support

## 2. BALAVA

### I. General Characteristics :

a. This Karana too is very auspicious & the natives good looking & spiritual. Any benefic Yoga from this Karana Lord lasts long – 18 years. They get lasting wealth.

b. They are like a Tiger, with quality variance as per this descending order: **Tiger – Leopard – Cat** in that order

c. Rearing of cats in house – indicates Balava

d. Slaves **of Gram/Vana Devatas, Kshetra Balakas** like Bhairava.

e. They always keep smiling without any valid reasons (sort of sheepish smile)

f. They like to smell every object – Tiger likes the smell of blood

g. They don't like to wear the same attire for long – hence frequent changeovers

h. They are very agile & fast – travel a lot on pilgrimage etc.

i. They are very systematic & disciplined Viz – Regular exercises, 6 times pooja, sports etc.

j. They are good in planning & professions relating to that are favorable. They may also indulge in professions not so much in practice/not in conformity with practicality.

k. Never develop any enmity with a **Balava** Native – They are highly vindictive. If inevitable, don't pardon & let them go and leave traces of their destruction – It will rebound with a vengeance later.

l. They reward sycophancy – Good way to extract gifts from them

m. They love treasures and pleasures.

n. They are bold, adventurous, take risks & succeed. They sacrifice for others & are liberal and caring.

o. They run & support charitable institutions like orphanage, old age homes etc. They care for their relations and joint families.

p. They are good in sports esp. games without arms-like kabaddi/karate/wrestling etc.

q. They are prone to skin ailments & mental fears

r. Those Balava Natives with Rahu in lagna are prone to ailments during MERCURY Dasha.

s. Balava Karana – Deactivates Doshas in horoscopes Viz Sarpa Dosha (Rahu in 2/5/7/8 etc.) & hence not much marital, progeny issues. This removes Manglik Dosha as well.

t. Worship of female deities is very helpful. Better if the deities are made of clay.

u. Medicine: Natives medicines prepared in crucibles through kiln process etc. works well for them (Man pudam/Burnt Clay etc.)

v.   If the Prashna Kundli for lost items – indicates Balava Karana – the thief is most likely to get caught

w.   This is a good Muhurta for Prayer/settling of long standing issues – Loan/Divorce etc.

II.   Worship Details

| Table 2 | | | | | |
|---|---|---|---|---|---|
| Balava Karana – Devata's and other Associated Items for Remedy & Worship | | | | | |
| Description | Associated Deities/Items | | SL No | Description | Associated Deities/Items |
| Ruling Planet | Rahu/*Moon | | 8 | Paste/ Powder | Chandan/ (Sandal) |
| Vara | Monday/Friday | | 9 | Cloth (Vastram) | Red |
| Athi Davata | Lord Brahma | | 10 | Gemstone | Pearl |
| Deities | Gram Devatas Ayyappa Vana Durga | | 11 | Dhoop | Add Sandal Powder |
| Animal | Tiger | | 12 | Metal/Vessel | Silver |
| Dhanya-Cereal | Arhar/Toor Dhal Red Gram | | 13 | Flower | SHENBAGAM/ Champaka Flower |
| Food/ Naivedhya | Kheer/Payasam (Pudding) | | 14 | Idol/Portrait | Deities with Tiger |

*Other traditions

III.   **Remedies:**

a.   Regular Pooja to Deities – using the above tabulated pooja-samagri like Sandal Abishek, Snan, Alankar, Archana, Doop, Deep & Naivedhya and Namaskar. This strengthens the Karana Lord.

b.  Donate Kheer/Payasam to temple for Prasad & Distribute to devotees

## 3. KAULAVA

### I. General Characteristics:

a.  The Natives are selfish & possessive. They are good people but have some self – destructive/negative traits as well

b.  They earn well through Govt contracts. They think less but act more. They serve in Govt and love that prestige/status.

c.  They do well in jobs under the earth like mines; bore well, digging-earth work etc.

d.  They are intelligent but ruthless in extracting work from others. Hence normally don't have a good image.

e.  Also, Kaulava males are selfish & extract lot of work from their spouse.

f.  They love their parents & also maintain good Aachara/ cleanliness

g.  They tend to have many children

h.  Also have more landed properties/Vehicles than their parents

i.  Kaulava Parent : Acts as yogi for one child & but Avayogi for another child

j.  Karana in Gandanta (@0° degree) – indicates special property – like it can make the native super rich etc.

k.  Gift Silver Anklets to your lady love/spouse for sustaining relationship

## II. MUHURTHA

a. It is Auspicious for all Muhurta
b. Good for purchase of Gold & Savings
c. Not good for selling of Land ( *Good for purchase)
d. Deva Prashna chart in Kaulava: Indicates that they have not performed Kunkum (vermilion) Archana for the Deity(A Dosha)
e. Good for activities under the ground – Foundation, Bore well, Granite etc.

## III. REMEDIES (Pooja & Rituals during this Karana)

a. They should always keep Red Sindhur on the forehead (Ayur Vriddhi-Longevity)
b. Mars in 8H: Perform Kunkum Archana (remedy from accidents etc.)
c. Gifting Kunkum Chimil(Saffron kit)is auspicious & beneficial
d. Bilva powder + Dhoop aarti – for shedding Karmic baggage during Kaulava. Beneficial for reducing the impact of Karma Nakshatra like Uttrabhadrapada etc.
e. Anybody having, planets in Karma Nakshatras in the Natal chart – Should perform this to reduce karmic load
f. Taking water in copper vessel reduces hypertension & suicidal tendency
g. Can donate Silver-Kavach to energize the deity for protection
h. Exalted Venus in a child's chart increases the longevity of the grandma (Donating Silver adds more years)
i. If there is any dispute between the trustees of a temple – installation of the deity made in copper – resolves the conflict

j. Worship of Bhu_Varaha (Varaha Avatar of Vishnu) at Sri Mushnam, Tamilnadu helps in getting benefits from Govt/Politics and Mental peace.

k. In general, detailed pooja with the indicated samagri – procedure, strengthens the KL to deliver results. Thus even if they encounter hurdles – still they get their work done fairly smoothly

## IV. Worship Details

| Table 3 | | | | | |
|---|---|---|---|---|---|
| Kaulava Karana – Devata's and other Associated Items for Remedy & Worship | | | | | |
| SL No | Description | Associated Deities/Items | SL No | Description | Associated Deities/Items |
| 1 | Ruling Planet | Saturn/*Mars | 8 | Paste/ Powder | Kunkum Saffron |
| 2 | Vara | Saturday/ *Tuesday | 9 | Cloth (Vastram) | Kandangi saree |
| 3 | Athi Davata | SURYA | 10 | Gemstone | Coral/ silver??? |
| 4 | Deities | Bhu_Varaha Varahi Subhramanya Mitra | 11 | Dhoop | Sambrani. + Bilva Powder |
| 5 | Animal | PIG/Swine | 12 | Metal/ Vessel | Silver (copper for water) |
| 6 | Dhanya-Cereal | Arhar/Toor Dhal Red Gram | 13 | Flower | Magizham Flower (Maulsari) |
| 7 | Food/ Naivedhya | Paniyaram (Appam) Sweet in SP Spicy in KP | 14 | Idol/Portrait | Earthen Pot Varahi Amman |

*Other traditions

❖ ❖ ❖

## 4. TAITULA

### I. General Characteristics :

a. This Karana is Highly Auspicious for Weddings

b. They long for Titles (before their names etc.). They also focus on the Title of a Book than its contents

c. Tendency to indulge in thefts & in secrecy

d. Taitula is well supported by Vanija-Controls its tendency to commit crimes, including 2$^{nd}$ marriage etc.

e. They are loyal & hard working. They do better in working for/under others

f. This favours females more than the male natives.

g. Hence, they succeed in profession if done in female's name or female related ones. Favours female entrepreneurs & the shops run by them are always crowded

h. They also focuses more on exterior beauty & entrance – but not so good inside

i. KP(Krishna Paksha)Taitula – Helps succeed through short-cuts

j. They carry the entire load of their family on their back (Donkey) & are soft hearted.

k. They don't execute their power/influence and always resolve the conflicts diplomatically & softly

l. They are steadfast, consistent, focused and hence easily overcome challenges. They need constant stimulus to succeed.

m. They generally seek secure jobs/professions and are also very frugal. Many work in Govt/Govt related departments.

n. They are very lustful & even get attracted to not so good looking.

o. They get to achieve results despite hurdles

## II. MUHURTHA

a.  It is excellent for Morning Muhurta & worship.
b.  Good for ladies to commence business – like fancy stores, artifacts etc.
c.  Good for Partying, Engagement and Luxury items

## III. REMEDIES (Pooja & Rituals during this Karana)

a.  Donate steel on Saturday, Shani Hora & Taitula Karana for Karmic Debt removal
b.  If Prashna Kundli – reveals Taitula, fix or donate steel vessels, handles etc. to temple
c.  Wearing yellow clothes is beneficial
d.  Donate Jasmine flower to homa & to temples
e.  Good Nimittha (augury) if they see a Jasmine vendor/ get Appam Prasad/Ayyappa Prasad without effort. Also, if they encounter anyone wearing Diamond/ its-name/yellow dresses/Iron-steel merchant – all indicate Karana Lords presence in support.
f.  Regular pooja with Snan/Abishek/Alankar/Archana/ Dhoop-Deepa & Naivedhya to the deities as mentioned in the Table-4 strengthens KL to deliver results.

I. Worship Details

| Table 4 | | | | | |
|---|---|---|---|---|---|
| Taitula Karana – Devata's and other Associated Items for Remedy & Worship | | | | | |
| SL No | Description | Associated Deities/Items | SL No | Description | Associated Deities/Items |
| 1 | Ruling Planet | Venus/ *Mercury | 8 | Paste/ Powder | Korozanai (cow_Bezor) |
| 2 | Vara | Wednesday | 9 | Cloth (Vastram) | Yellow Cloth |
| 3 | Athi Devata | Vishnu Narayana (Pitris), Aditya | 10 | Gemstone | Diamond |
| 4 | Deities | Jyeshta Devi Ranganatha Aditya | 11 | Dhoop | Sambrani. Add Turmeric Powder- Vangipattai |
| 5 | Animal | Donkey | 12 | Metal/Vessel | Silver (Vessel Iron) |
| 6 | Dhanya- Cereal | | 13 | Flower | Jasmine |
| 7 | Food/ Naivedhya | Appam | 14 | Idol/Portrait | Jyeshta Devi Lakshmi Narayan |

*Other traditions

## 5. GARAJA(GAR)

### I. General Characteristics :

a. All Males wedded to a Garaja female are assured of progeny (Putra Bhagya)

b.  They should always keep a twin elephant (statute or picture – they represent Dad& Son)

c.  They always think of the opposite sex, thereby face issues lifelong/all of a sudden. Need to be cautious in opposite sex matters to sustain peace.

d.  They copulate at the most appropriate time – Results in progeny

e.  Excepting the transit phases over Rahu – Ketu, the ladies can get pregnant easily

f.  They can rise from rags to riches.

g.  Bit Hyper-tensive. Tend to put on weight due to excessive eating

h.  They are public welfare conscious & take up, highlight the people's issues to the Govt attention.

i.  They are active in spiritual, religious activities & are attracted to the knowledgeable and scholarly.

j.  They are systematic & time conscious.

k.  Good at planning & endowed with the gift of the gab- Good orators

l.  Get good success over competitors & Muhurta supports success in elections

m.  They get favours from Govt, success in competition. They are Charitable too.

n.  Good at Counseling – but still better through the medium of stories & lyrics.

o.  Creative mind & hence successful in all creative arts like Painting/dance etc. and derive happiness from them.

p.  Virile & hence good at sperm donation

q.  Make good Gynecologists

r.  Astros born in Garaja – are experts in suggesting solution for childless issues

s. Agriculture & Farming is favorable for them

t. They can prolong the life of any person in their vicinity.

u. They sustain their lineage & become happy grand parents

## II. **MUHURTHA**

a. Garaja Karana is a good Muhurta for competitive examinations

b. Also good for farming & sowing activities.

c. The Centre part of this Karana (42-62%) is the most auspicious for removal of Putra dosha

d. Good for all surgical procedures – Study of Medicine and Agriculture

e. Good for any business – water related including Milk dairy etc.

f. Saturn if in LD (Lowest Degree) & posited in the star of Mars – Grants easy access to landed property. Such a native if born in Garaja Karana – will develop & multiply that by many folds

g. Note: Taitula(Donkey) with Elephant(Garaja), Garaja with Tiger – (Balava) will cause separation & love failure

h. Mars & Ketu if connected to the 12H by Conjunction/ Aspect – indicate the possibility of Dur-Marana & multiple deaths. Sincere Prayers & Worships in Garaja Muhurta – prevents such mishaps & premature deaths

## III.  Worship Details

| Table 5 | | | | | |
|---|---|---|---|---|---|
| Garaja Karana – Devata's and other Associated Items for Remedy & Worship | | | | | |
| SL No | Description | Associated Deities/ Items | SL No | Description | Associated Deities/Items |
| 1 | Ruling Planet | Moon/ *Jupiter | 8 | Paste/ Powder | Kasu katti (Herbal powder Extract from Betalnut) |
| 2 | Vara | Thursday | 9 | Cloth (Vastram) | Black Cloth |
| 3 | Athi Davata | Guru/ Dakshina Murthy | 10 | Gemstone | Yellow Sapphire |
| 4 | Deities | Vinayaka (Pillayarpatti) Bhoo Devi | 11 | Dhoop | Neela Kundumani Powder in Dhoop |
| 5 | Animal | Elephant | 12 | Metal/Vessel | Lead |
| 6 | Dhanya-Cereal | Chole | 13 | Flower | Hibiscus |
| 7 | Food/ Naivedhya | Raw Cow Milk | 14 | Idol/Portrait | Twin Elephant or Ganapathy |

*Other traditions

## IV.  Remedies

a. Beneficial to keep Elephant idol/photo in house prominently-even in door frames etc.

b. Temples with Elephant sculpture – reflect Garaja Karana impact. Any problem in this Karana gets relieved if we worship god in Gajamoksha sthals

c. Donate Prasad of cooked Milk-Rice/Kheer after worship. Also, Keep KL in pooja room.
d. Donate black clothes to Ayyappa bhakts/Local deities like Karuppu/Bhairava etc.
e. Regular worship with the above pooja-samagri viz. Snan, Abishek, Alankar, Archana, Dhoop, Deepa & Naivedhya and prayers to the above deities will strengthen the KL. Thus the promised delays/hurdles are overcome.

# 6. VANIJA

## I. **General Characteristics :**

a. The Natives born in Vanija Karana, generally prosper in trade/business
b. Trade/business is inborn & they possess convincing conversation ability. Mostly successful in Trade.
c. They are good in planning & admin and are very calculative & business oriented
d. They should treat their mother well – Must refrain from incurring the wrath of mother – If not, no easy redemption
e. They tend to easily fall in love, possible multiple love affairs
f. They possess lovable nature. They continue their love affairs even at the place of their work/profession – Prone to consequential problems therefrom
g. They should worship Shiva at Thirumalaipadi temple (to Suppress the excess desire)
h. Not good for partnership business – They should go alone as they are not good team players

   i. Extravaganza is their forte. Their speeches are highly imaginary, not much in others – public welfare.

   j. Their Speech is bit harsh

   k. Helps overcome the impacts of Thithi Shunya in Horoscope

   l. Lucky charm for VANIJA is Kaulava Karana guys

  m. Not good for individual Morality

   n. This Karana – gives sustained effect for longer duration (Whether good or bad)

## II. MUHURTHA

   a. Good Muhurta for Ayur(Longevity) & Aishwaryam(Wealth)

   b. Auspicious for Dosha dissolution

   c. Good for farming, agriculture & digging bore well

   d. Good for Medical treatment – General not surgery

   e. Deepa worship & by Aarti is beneficial

   f. Worship Gaja Lakshmi for wealth

   g. Good to commence business & trade

   h. Feed cows esp. on Friday/Sunday

   i. Vanija Karana imparts a lasting impact – Viz most famous temples are founded in Vanija

   j. Vanija : restores the ancient temple (Life inducing Karana)

   k. Karana activates Fortuna point to give wealth

## III. Worship Details

| Table 6 | | | | | |
|---------|---|---|---|---|---|
| Vanija Karana – Devata's and other Associated Items for Remedy & Worship | | | | | |
| SL No | Description | Associated Deities/Items | SL No | Description | Associated Deities/Items |
| 1 | Ruling Planet | Sun/*Venus | 8 | Paste/ Powder | Turmeric |
| 2 | Vara | Sunday/ *Friday | 9 | Cloth (Vastram) | Woolen Cloth |
| 3 | Athi Devata | Lakshmi-on lotus Seat, Shri Devi | 10 | Gemstone | (Diamond) |
| 4 | Deities | Gaja Lakshmi Shiva worship- Thirumalaipadi Temple | 11 | Dhoop | Add Shank Bhasma Powder in Dhoop |
| 5 | Animal | COW in SP Bull in KP (Nandi) | 12 | Metal/Vessel | Pancha Lokam |
| 6 | Dhanya-Cereal | | 13 | Flower | Shankh pushpa Nilochana Flower |
| 7 | Food/ Naivedhya | CURD or Curd Rice | 14 | Idol/Portrait | Akshaya Patra Tarasu (Weighing Scale) |

*Other traditions

## IV. Remedies

a. Worship during Pradosha Kaal(Trayodashi before sunset) is the most beneficial remedy

b. Go-Dhana/Kamadhenu idol to the deserving

   c.  Matru-Seva & refraining from causing hurt to others

   d.  Donate water, butter milk to others in summer

   e.  Regular worship with the above pooja-samagri viz. Snan, Abishek, Alankar, Archana, Dhoop, Deepa & Naivedhya and prayers to the above deities will strengthen the KL. Thus, the promised delays/hurdles are overcome.

## 7. BHADRA(VISHTI)

### I. General Characteristics :

a. **Bhadra** Karana: (It is Vishti in North & most of these observations apply to Vishti too (In TN – Vishti is considered only as a part of Bhadra – later phase)

b. Bhadra is a Maraka – second only to Mandhi (an Upa Graha) in inflicting losses of wealth & life and destruction. They are prone to get angry easily

c. The Natives born in Bhadra are fairly free from afflictions indicated by Ketu in their Natal charts

d. They are very deep down in their mind. Always agitating/scratching their mind like a hen

e. No secret should be shared with them – Lest they pass it on to others

f. Mars & VE if conjunct in 3H in general – indicates Doubting Thomases. Bhadra Natives with such a conjunction are good for espionage & intelligence duties like Spies and Investigation officers

g. If they have their Ascendant in a Ketu star & if Ketu is in an Angle (Trikona) – Easily attain Yoga/Mantra Vidhya Siddhi.

h. Natives born in Shukla-Paksha Bhadra – excel in Research & Investigative journalism. Also in Crime Investigation Department & help in resolution

i.  Natives born in Krishna-Paksha Bhadra – just investigate, find faults & abuse and fight with those at fault – but don't rectify or help in resolution. Prone to indulge in not so good acts

j.  Always in needs – in Eternity. There is no Bhadra Karana Guy whose needs are satisfied in full

k.  They keep searching for jobs in perpetuity

l.  Always short of liquid cash/in need of money. Poverty is a possibility too.

m.  Their search is never ending & they keep running after something elusive. They work hard without rest.

n.  They always harp on the Negatives experienced & easily forget their good & joyous Moments

o.  Can neutralize poison – evil and bring good fortune. Can provide a lucky charm. Also if they give Vibhuti after Mantra – helps remove poison from body.

p.  Favorable Karana for getting a progeny.

q.  They are good in sculpture, painting etc.

r.  They progress better by annihilating competition. Good far waging war & mass destruction. Even farmers of this Karana-use pesticides & immediately destroy harmful insects

s.  This is true if the Prashna chart indicates Bhadra with Saturn+ Mercury conjunction

t.  Susceptible to eye ailments/leg Pain.

u.  They are good for employment as subordinates – but refrain from engaging them in cash handling

v.  They are also misers & fickle minded

w.  Quick disenchantment/fatigue in marital life. Prone to losses of wealth after marriage

x.  They do better abroad/outside the native state. May live far away from family to earn for comforts

y. They take good care of their family despite hardships. They are highly patriotic too

z. More on Bhadra
   - ✓ They maintain their body well & take care to present themselves well
   - ✓ Never marry a partner with hormonal issues. They are prone to infertility.
   - ✓ Should refrain from taking chicken meat
   - ✓ Difficulty in completing the task as planned & delays are normal.
   - ✓ They easily get disillusioned & need constant motivation to succeed.
   - ✓ Endowed with ESP – Power
   - ✓ They possess good Artistic expression & taste: good beauticians, skilled at embroidery & painting etc. Also quest for knowledge.
   - ✓ They make good doctors & chemists
   - ✓ Prostration & surrender – pays off, in winning them over
   - ✓ Bhadra reduces the negatives of Thithi Shunya

## II. MUHURTHA

a. This Karana Muhurta is favorable to commence learning Occult Vidhya.

b. Good for Medical treatment – Esp. Skin diseases

c. If the Anughya (Seeking Permission) is in Bhadra in Deva Prashna – The Astrologer should not proceed further. That temple indicates destruction.

d. Not auspicious for timing of birth through caesarian operation

e. Not auspicious for marriage & for Prashna.

f. Not Favorable for Farming & Agriculture. May result in heavy losses-even if they farm on a fertile land

g. Note: Bhadra-Vishti: Supports progress by destruction of opposition

Ex: Congress Mukt Bharat slogan – 24/14/14 KP – Dashami (8.20-19.10 hours). NAMO filed his nomination at 2.02pm and declared his intent for a Congress Mukt Bharat.

## III. MORE ABOUT VISHTI

a. Vishti is a Female – Daughter of SUN & hence SATURN's sibling

b. No staring/Kama drishti at a Vishti Girl – Dangerous

c. Any Shraap/Curse spelt in Vishti gives intense effect

d. Giving Thamboolam(Betal leaves help in mitigation)

e. They are beautiful but have harsh temperament

f. Vishti determines the Loka, the departed soul has travelled to-in a Death chart

g. If Moon is in Aries/Taurus/Gemini/Scorpio – Madam Vishti will transport the Soul to Swarga – not much need to give Shrardh

h. If Moon in Virgo/Libra/Sagittarius/Capricorn – Gets transported to Pathal Loka (Rebirth certain)

i. If Moon in Cancer/Leo/Aquarius/Pisces-Back in Earth, Bhu-Loka, Rebirth certain

j. Go to the respective temples for prayers/remedy with deity looking accordingly

    Urdhva Mukha (Eyes up) – Heaven

    Adho Mukham (Eyes Down) – Pathal

    Sama Mukham (Eyes Straight) – Earth

k. Vastu Purusha is her Commander in Chief

l. Vishti Karana timings occur in the later part of Chaturdashi, Ekadashi, Purnima, and Shukla Ashtami.

m. Not auspicious for any Muhurta

n.  Vishti gives Kapha(phlegm) & sinusitis

o.  For Vishti Dosha – Shiva worship & Bilva powder Dhoop helps

p.  Vishti Deities : Bhadra Kaali, Bhairavi, Kala Ratri, Kaali-64 Rupas, Shooli, Rudri & Maha Maayi

I.  **Worship Details**

| Table 7 | | | | | |
|---|---|---|---|---|---|
| Bhadra Karana – Devata's and other Associated Items for Remedy & Worship | | | | | |
| SL No | Description | Associated Deities/Items | SL No | Description | Associated Deities/Items |
| 1 | Ruling Planet | Ketu/ *Saturn | 8 | Paste/ Powder | Pachai Karpooram/ Edible Camphor |
| 2 | Vara | Saturday/ Tuesday | 9 | Cloth (Vastram) | Animal Skin (Tiger/Deer) |
| 3 | Athi Devata | Yama/ Dharma raj | 10 | Gemstone | Pukhraj/Yellow Sapphire |
| 4 | Deities | Subhramanya (Trichendur), Kala Bhairava in KP | 11 | Dhoop | Rose Powder in Dhoop |
| 5 | Animal | Hen | 12 | Metal/ Vessel | Bronze (Elliptical shape) |
| 6 | Dhanya-Cereal | | 13 | Flower | Kundumani poo/Rosary pea flower |
| 7 | Food/ Naivedhya | Mixed Rice-Chitranna | 14 | Idol/Portrait | Subhramanya-Shiva-Bhairava/ Bhairavi |

*Other traditions

> Regular worship with the above pooja-samagri viz. Snan, Abishek, Alankar, Archana, Dhoop, Deepa & Naivedhya and prayers to the above deities will strengthen the KL. Thus the promised delays/hurdles are overcome.

## 8. SHAKUNI

### I. General Characteristics :

a. This is a Malefic Karana – Helps in Black magic etc.

b. The Shakuni Karana natives are intelligent but passive. Also Practical, bold & prosperous – even if they are not, show themselves as one

c. Highly intuitive and hence take right decisions.

d. They refine themselves faster

e. They are very Tactful and Cunning too

f. Supports doctors and politicians in career. Like to work in Jewelry field

g. Shakuni Karana + Rahu in Lagna portends Mortgage of things/property in perpetuity

h. Thithi Shunya is more virulent for these Natives. Very painful

i. Intelligent but Cowardly – May indulge in anonymous petitioning

j. Good in eviction of opponents/win over opposition (By clever design).

k. Good in planning (from the back end). Also good for fighting for truth

l. They are ruthless in punishing the guilty – even drive away people and desist from any reconciliation process

m. They use strong/harsh language. May cause separation too.

n. They are prone to take loans on high interest/mortgage etc.

o. They should not take up unfamiliar works without right assistance. May cause closure.

p. This supports closure of any business – Hence No commencement or engagement of the guys of this Karana in crucial posts

## II. MUHURTHA

a. Auspicious for treatment of internal diseases with Medicine – tablets etc.

b. Auspicious to take up work – promising glory

c. Inauspicious for mortgage, loans etc.

d. Not auspicious for purchase of properties – May land up in documentation issues

e. (General Tips: Remedy for Graha Dosha – The star adjacent to the star in which the dosha planet is placed – helps)

f. Long pending works can be done in Shakuni

g. Good For Closure of any long pending cases/Disputes

## III.  Worship Details

| Table 8 | | | | | |
|---|---|---|---|---|---|
| Shakuni Karana – Devata's and other Associated Items for Remedy & Worship | | | | | |
| SL No | Description | Associated Deities/Items | SL No | Description | Associated Deities/Items |
| 1 | Ruling Planet | Saturn/*Rahu | 8 | Paste/ Powder | Sandal Turmeric mix/ Vibhuti(ash) |
| 2 | Vara | Saturday | 9 | Cloth (Vastram) | SP:Newcloth KP: Old Cloth Blue/Black |
| 3 | Athi Davata | Vishnu | 10 | Gemstone | Neelam/Royal Blue Sapphire |
| 4 | Deities | Kala Bhairava Shaneswara (Thirunallar) | 11 | Dhoop | Akil Kattai/ Aloe Wood |
| 5 | Animal | Crow/Owl | 12 | Metal/ Vessel | Stone Vessel |
| 6 | Dhanya-Cereal | Sesame | 13 | Flower | Shenbagam (Champaka) |
| 7 | Food/ Naivedhya | Jaggery Cones (sesame rice for Crow) | 14 | Idol/Portrait | Stree Vishnu (Mohini) Palm Leave Scriptures |

***Other traditions**

## IV.  Remedies

a.  Feeding of Crows

b.  Visit Shaneswar temple at Thirunallar wearing old clothes – Donate garland with black thread

c.  Donate sweet pongal (jiggery-rice) as Prasad/Offering.

d. Regular worship (whenever planning auspicious work/to get something) with the above pooja-samagri viz. Snan, Abishek, Alankar, Archana, Dhoop, Deepa & Naivedhya and prayers to the above deities will strengthen the KL. Thus, the possible delays/hurdles are overcome.

❖ ❖ ❖

## 9. NAGAVA

I. **General Characteristics:**

a. This is a Hardcore Malefic Karana. This is VISHA-RAHU, a poisonous one.

b. This Karana denotes Snakes/Serpents. There are multiple varieties of snakes & so are these natives with multiple gunas/types of character.

c. Nagava Natives are good orators & philosophers

d. Those who Market & Sell by Voice/Shouting – **Nagava Karana**

e. Priests especially Fathers in church

f. Very Egoistic – value self-esteem. Like sycophancy

g. Research oriented – investigative mind.

h. Target Oriented – Never mind chasing & running after their love till they win over them

i. Good Miners – Digging wells, mining of gold, related businesses etc.

j. Excel in medicine, carpentry, sculpture, magic, tiles work, cake shop, bore well/well, lathe, marketing

k. They display lot of good qualities – like good in Serpent-vasya, Anesthesia's etc. If well directed can become a Gynani (wise men)

l. They can survive anywhere – Can transform adversity into prosperity. They are highly suspicious too

m. Revolutionary – Rowdy elements & Extremists and also fight for good causes.

n. They don't look for perfections in their partners – like they can marry a person who is already married and so on.

o. Copulation with a Nagava Karana Partner involves High Risk of contracting STD – diseases. Hence need moderation.

p. Nagava Karana makes one Vakri – with Planets Doubly Vakri (More Noise).

q. Their look/vision resembles that of a snake

r. They are prone to skin diseases like pigmentation of skin

s. Nagava Karana with Nodes in 6H in an Airy sign – Indicates a lasting skin disease

t. Voracious Eaters – No tongue control. Remedy is worshiping Saints in Samadhi, Brindavan)

u. Mannerism: They repeat their conversation/speeches!

v. Hence, they are good at magic/tantra and marketing

w. They display high sense of Loyalty to those who helped/fed them.

x. They change their character every six months. Gochara RAHU is beneficial for them

y. Nagava natives with Rahu in 5H, generally worship Samadhi-Brindavan of saints

z. Good for Detox – Removal of Toxins – Implies such Doctors too

## II. MUHURTHA

a. If Prashna Kundali is in Nagava – indicates that the Native can survive anywhere

   b. Nagava Karana with Nodes in Trine (1/5/9) – Indicates a Samadhi/Grave in the house.

   c. Good for worship of Samadhi-Brindavan of saints

## III. Worship Details

| Table 9 | | | | | |
|---|---|---|---|---|---|
| Nagava Karana – Devata's and other Associated Items for Remedy & Worship | | | | | |
| SL No | Description | Associated Deities/Items | SL No | Description | Associated Deities/Items |
| 1 | Ruling Planet | Rahu/*Ketu | 8 | Paste/ Powder | Wooden powder Mixed |
| 2 | Vara | Friday | 9 | Cloth (Vastram) | Tree Barks |
| 3 | Athi Devata | Sarpa Devata like Vasuki, Nagaraja, Adi Sesha | 10 | Gemstone | Vaidooriyam (Lapis Lazuli) /Cats Eye |
| 4 | Deities | Nagaraja Aditya | 11 | Dhoop | Dhoop Sambrani/ Loban |
| 5 | Animal | Snake | 12 | Metal/ Vessel | Stone-vessel/ any |
| 6 | Dhanya-Cereal | | 13 | Flower | Olai poo |
| 7 | Food/ Naivedhya | Ghee Ghee Rice | 14 | Idol/Portrait | Flute Siddhar (Pambatti) Any Naga Devata (Manasa Devi) |

*Other traditions

### IV. **Remedies**

a. Donate Cow-ghee to Yagna for Karma removal. Also donate Cow-ghee by weight or 10% of their weight at least

b. Donate Vaidooriyam Mala (Lapis Lazuli) to temple deities for karma removal. Also do Mantra Japa(Meditate)with this mala

c. Donate Sambrani/Loban Dhoop to temples

d. Regular worship (whenever planning auspicious work/to get something) with the above pooja-samagri viz. Snan, Abishek, Alankar, Archana, Dhoop, Deepa & Naivedhya and prayers to the above deities will strengthen the KL. Thus, the promised delays/hurdles are overcome.

## 10. CHATUSHPADA

### I. **General Characteristics :**

a. This is a STHIRA Karana & is quite a malefic one-This occurs during Amavasya.

b. This troubles Leo/Taurus Lagna-Rashi guys more

c. **Chatushpada** – Means a Four Legged one – An Animal – Mainly a Dog

d. These Natives have a high sense of Security – like a Canine

e. Very possessive of knowledge-They preserve whatever knowledge they receive

f. They are highly pre-emptive characters – Anticipate problems in advance

g. They don't get help from Jupiter(guru) if it's in Thithi Shunya at the time of their birth – even if it's in good strength/dignity

h.  High Loyalty/Truthful/Hard working – but take liberty to occupy or share their boss's seat. They start earning when young

i.  Security Related Professions like Police& Military suits them – but only in Commanding positions

j.  Many get irritated with them without reasons

k.  They are fitness conscious – Good at Gyms

l.  They detest control, love freedom. Hence may pursue independent work

m.  Excel in Multi-Tasking. Get good fame & status

n.  Highly Sexed – Multiple Relationships (if Mars – Venus in close conjunction). Don't Match with (Hen/Crow)

o.  They don't save much – Expend a lot for upkeep of Honour & Dignity

p.  They honor their promises – Male Natives dole out more promises

q.  Good at Research on Occultism & Philosophy.

## II.  MUHURTHA

a.  Should be avoided for auspicious events (Shub Karya)

b.  The Karana Lord does not support Speculation like Trading in Share Market etc.

c.  Good Karana for Performing Shrardh(Rituals) to ancestors (Esp. if it's on Tuesday/Thursday) – Guarantees Moksha for them

d.  Good for any Security related work

e.  If Ashta Mangala Prashna (Deva Prashna) is in this Karana – It indicates the presence of an unsatisfied Jeeva – warrants remedial measures

f.  Ex.: Mars+ Ketu conjunction in a dual sign – indicates Pisashcha Yoga – Remedy by giving Shrardh in Chatushpada

g. Note: In Deva Prashna such a combo indicates that the – Balalayam for the old Murthi (Vigraha) is not maintained properly.

## III. Worship Details

| Table 10 | | | | | |
|---|---|---|---|---|---|
| Chatushpada Karana – Devata's and other Associated Items for Remedy & Worship | | | | | |
| SL No | Description | Associated Deities/Items | SL No | Description | Associated Deities/Items |
| 1 | Ruling Planet | Jupiter/Mars in-SP/KP respectively *Rahu | 8 | Paste/ Powder | Vibhuti/Sacred Ash |
| 2 | Vara | Thursday | 9 | Cloth (Vastram) | Dress of Leaves/Cotton cloth |
| 3 | Athi Devata | Mani Bhadra (Kubera's Chieftain) | 10 | Gemstone | Spatikam (Crystal) |
| 4 | Deities | Rudra Bhairav at Kshetrapala puram | 11 | Dhoop | Sandal Powder |
| 5 | Animal | Dog | 12 | Metal/ Vessel | Wooden |
| 6 | Dhanya-Cereal | | 13 | Flower | Kondrai Poo(Golden Shower – Flower) |
| 7 | Food/ Naivedhya | Honey | 14 | Idol/ Portrait | Wooden Spatula (Keep Bhairava Pic at the outer Entrance) |

***Other traditions**

## IV. **Remedies**

a. Vrat & Fasting – on Amavasya/Purnima, Ashtami Thithi is an effective remedy. Must Refrain from Copulation too.

b. Donation/Sponsorship for Temple security like Doors/Compound walls gates etc. – But in Anonymity

c. Worship the Karana Lord (KL) on Bharani Nakshatra/Tuesday

d. Regular worship (whenever planning auspicious work/to get something) with the above pooja-samagri viz. Snan, Abishek, Alankar, Archana, Dhoop, Deepa & Naivedhya and prayers to the above deities will strengthen the KL. Thus, the promised delays/hurdles are overcome.

## 11. **KINSTUGHNA**

### I. **General Characteristics :**

a. This is also a STHIRA Karana & is quite a Malefic one – occurs during Amavasya.

b. If born in Shukla Paksha (Waxing Phase of Moon) – Make it to Higher Studies in Medicine

c. If in Krishna Paksha – too Study Medicine, but at a lower level

d. Their 3rd House in chart is afflicted normally

e. They take care of their parents & siblings

f. Any event happening in this Karana – its impact lasts for 3 days viz. Any greeting/kissing (+ve) or even a curse (-ve) gets impacted in mind for 3 days.

g. They retain Good memory – Memory waves

h. This signifies a worm/insect – when grown, a serpent

i. Those who are down and out – can seek resurrection/redemption of fortunes if trained under these Natives

j. Skilled in transforming Agricultural Lands – Improve their yield

k. Good for rearing silk worms/Dealing in Silk/Natural manure/Earth worms etc.

l. Good in Herbal medicines & cure

m. Also possess Negative thoughts – tend to believe that they hold memories of previous birth

n. Good for Tapas and Adhyatmik-Vidhya (Spirituality), if they refrain from bad company/habits. They can attain good Siddhi.

o. This Karana improves relationship after the birth of a child. They aspire to get more children(Rahu Nakshatras are in Kama Trikona)

p. They spread news (Indulge in most forwards in SM) and are well informed – Good at printing/publishing journals, advertising handouts etc. Good knowhow in Medicine, Herbs too.

## II. MUHURTHA

a. Good Muhurta for conciliation proceedings – Compromises Easier

b. This Karana is auspicious for Astrologers – To commence Study of Medical Astrology

c. Reconciliation with a warring spouse is possible with a single kiss during Kinstughna

d. Any mediation/discussion held during the first 1/3rd Muhurta ( 4 hours) will reach a positive conclusion

e. The Middle portion of Muhurta is good for improving the relationship quotient

f. If Deva Prashna chart has this Karana – Reflects that the temple is spoiled by termites

## III. Worship Details

| Table 11 | | | | | |
|---|---|---|---|---|---|
| Kinstughna Karana – Devata's and other Associated Items for Remedy & Worship | | | | | |
| SL No | Description | Associated Deities/Items | SL No | Description | Associated Deities/Items |
| 1 | Ruling Planet | Mercury/*Ketu | 8 | Paste/ Powder | Javadu Powder |
| 2 | Vara | Wednesday | 9 | Cloth (Vastram) | Only Tops (No full dress) |
| 3 | Athi Devata | Vayu Bhagwan | 10 | Gemstone | Pearl |
| 4 | Deities | Lakshmi Devi Dhanvantri, Vaithiswaran koil | 11 | Dhoop | Kungliyam (White Dammar) |
| 5 | Animal | Worm/Sarpa | 12 | Metal/ Vessel | Bamboo/Cane |
| 6 | Dhanya-Cereal | | 13 | Flower | Kongu |
| 7 | Food/ Naivedhya | Sugar | 14 | Idol/Portrait | Yoga Anjaneya |

*Other traditions

## IV. Remedies

a. Donate sugar by weight (Tulabaram (scale) dhan) in temples.

b. Suggested Remedy : Taking care of the Mentally Challenged

c. Rahu Dosha :Donate Sugar/Jaggery as weighed in Tulabaram or gift a pearl chain to a Temple

d. Regular worship (whenever planning auspicious work/to get something) with the above pooja-samagri viz. Snan,

Abishek, Alankar, Archana, Dhoop, Deepa & Naivedhya and prayers to the above deities will strengthen the KL. Thus, the promised delays/hurdles are overcome.

## 12. YOGI & KARANA LORD

- ✓ If the KL & YOGI planet are same – Very auspicious – Native is saved from harm
- ✓ If KL & YOGI planets are in a Trine – The MD/AD Dasha periods will not be problematic
- ✓ If KL is in Trine/Kendra to Lagna-good. If the lagna lord is in the Nakshatra of KL it's very good.
- ✓ If KL is Avayogi-he reduces its maleficence & if in Avayogi star-just delays-no denial.
- ✓ Yogi in KL Nakshatra – More Yogam. If Avayogi in KL Nakshatra some obstructions.
- ✓ Arthapragnan ( 1 1/2 Hours Period daily) is a Upa-Graha which indicates fatal period/diseases : KL helps minimizes its impact
- ✓ Karna Lord helps in weakening the adverse effects of Upagrahas like Mandhi, Arthapragnan etc.
- ✓ Ex: Arthapragnan – gives itching problems, dirty slang in speech etc. Keeping & Worshipping KL will help their mitigation
- ✓ If KL and Nodes are in same degree – Sarpa Dosha gets dissolved

## 13. GENERAL:

- ✓ Worship the deity in Pooja by decorating it, by the Ornament relevant to the Ruling Karana of the day – helps a lot! This Ensures that the Deity Starts living there permanently

✓ Transfer of Property/Inheritance should be in the Muhurta – When Your Karana Lord is not transiting your Karma Nakshatra! This way – the recipient does not inherit your Karma.

# CHAPTER 3

# YOGA

---

"AUM GAM GANAPATHAYE NAMAHA"

"AUM GURAVE NAMAHA"

## NAMA YOGAS

1. There are 2 types of Yogas generally used in Panchanga.

   ✓ One is called **Tatkallika Yoga(s)** – **Temporary/Current Yoga**, which is based on **Vaara** (Day of the week) and **Nakshatra** (Star of the day) combination – mainly checked before resorting to any activity.

   ✓ The other one is called **Nama Yoga** aka **Nithya Yoga**, which are based on the degrees (angular distance) of Moon & Sun. Each such yoga is determined whenever the Moon moves away from Sun by 13°20' degrees. Thus one yoga for each day, hence also called as **Nithya Yoga**.

2. These are also different from other Yogas like Bhava Yogas/ Graha Yogas used in Predictive Vedic Astrology. The **Nama Yoga** obtained at the birth time of the Native is reckoned as the Birth Yoga of the Native.

3. These **Nama Yogas** play a significant role in dealing with the afflictions and hence of immense help in **KARMA JYOTISH**

4. There are 27 **Nama Yogas** in total, Out of which some are extremely favorable, others moderately favorable& the remaining not so favorable. They are tabulated as under

| SL. NO | Namayoga Name | Yogi | Avayogi | Yoga signification |
|---|---|---|---|---|
| 1 | Vishkumbha | Saturn | Moon | Pot of Venom/support-Inauspicious* |
| 2 | Preeti | Mercury | Mars | Attachment, Fondness, Auspicious |
| 3 | Ayushman | Ketu | Rahu | Long Life – Moderately Auspicious* |
| 4 | Saubhagya | Venus | Jupiter | Fortunate-Lucky, Auspicious |
| 5 | Shobana | Sun | Saturn | Shining Splendor, Auspicious |
| 6 | Athiganda | Moon | Mercury | Very Strong knot, Danger-Inauspicious |

| 7 | Sukarma | Mars | Ketu | Good karma-Virtuous, Moderately Auspicious |
|---|---|---|---|---|
| 8 | Dhriti | Rahu | Venus | Fixed-Focused – Moderately Auspicious |
| 9 | Shoola | Jupiter | Sun | Sharp weapon, Pain – Inauspicious |
| 10 | Ganda | Saturn | Moon | Knot-Danger Inauspicious |
| 11 | Vriddhi | Mercury | Mars | Growth – Auspicious |
| 12 | Dhruva | Ketu | Rahu | Stable-Eternal Moderately Auspicious |
| 13 | Vyaghata | Venus | Jupiter | Blow/Beating – Inauspicious |
| 14 | Harshana | Sun | Saturn | Happy-Joy-Thrill, Moderately Auspicious |
| 15 | Vajra | Moon | Mercury | Thunderbolt-Diamond, Moderately Auspicious |
| 16 | Siddhi | Mars | Ketu | Success – Fruition, Auspicious |
| 17 | Vyatipata | Rahu | Venus | Destruction-Calamity Inauspicious |
| 18 | Variyan | Jupiter | Sun | Strong Ambition, Comfort, Moderately Auspicious |
| 19 | Parigha | Saturn | Moon | Iron bar-Obstruction, Inauspicious |
| 20 | Shiva | Mercury | Mars | Blissful, Auspicious |
| 21 | Siddha | Ketu | Rahu | Proven – Attained, Auspicious |
| 22 | Sadhya | Venus | Jupiter | Amenable-Accomplished, Moderately Auspicious |
| 23 | Shubha | Sun | Saturn | Radiates good, Auspicious |
| 24 | Shukla/ Subrahma | Moon | Mercury | Bright-White, Auspicious* |
| 25 | Brahma | Mars | Ketu | Wise, priest – Eternal Inauspicious |
| 26 | Indra-Mahendra | Rahu | Venus | Top class, Moderately Auspicious |
| 27 | Vaidhriti | Guru | Sun | Division/Partition, No support, Inauspicious |

Let us discuss each of the 27 Nama/Nithya Yogas in detail – Particularly how they play out wrt the Yogi-Avayogi phenomena, in the subsequent chapters.

## 1. Vishkumbha Yoga

| Yogi Star | Yogi | Avayogi Star | Avayogi |
|---|---|---|---|
| Pushya | Saturn | S'ravana | Moon |
| **Vishkumbha Characteristics** | | | |

They are born with Saturn (Pushya) as the Yogi and Moon as the Avayogi (S'ravana)

➢ Hence are promised some regular income & financial returns in proportion to the efforts put in.

➢ They are intuitive & independent – Have cordial relationship with their relatives

➢ Have – Intense sexual Desires and possibly land up in Problems through opposite sex

In General:

➢ This Yoga is not good for any Muhurta & No auspicious work could be undertaken in this yoga

➢ However the Natives born in this yoga are intelligent, beautiful, Charming and have a good family/Social circle

➢ They are Spiritual with interest in Occult and are intuitive

➢ They are born leaders and can accomplish their goals easily, amass huge wealth through business – Secured Economically

➢ They are independent, good looking and have a satisfactory family life

➢ They may walk side-on or with a bend

**This is a Malefic Yoga; Let us discuss few example charts**

A. **Example: 1** – Chart for a Native born **in Vishkumbha Yoga.**

| Lagna | | | |
|---|---|---|---|
| | | Vishkumbha | Jupiter |
| Moon | | | |
| | | | |

i. Lagna: Pisces, Moon in Capricorn – S'ravana Nakshatra, Jupiter in Cancer-Pushya Nakshatra. Accordingly Saturn is the Yogi and Moon is the Avayogi. Running Dasha at Birth (MD) – Moon

ii. Lagna-Lord (LL), Jupiter is exalted and also in the Nakshatra of Yogi. Hence it promises a great yoga for the native and also the power to withstand & neutralize the malefic impact of other planets.

iii. The Avayogi Moon is posited in 8H from the 4H. This portends high affliction to Mother in terms of Health/Pain and even danger to life. As the Birth star of the Native is at 8th house – 8H from the 4th house (signifying Mother), it inflicts high Maraka effect to his mother & family – despite the 5th lord(5L) Moon placed at the house of gains-11H from Lagna during its MD.

iv. **This is because Moon, despite being a Purva-Punya house lord – 5L, is an Avayogi for the Native. Thus the Avayogi deprives the native from enjoying the fruits of his past gains/yogam.**

v. Let us assume that another planet is placed in either Rohini/Hasta/S'ravana – the Nakshatra of moon. This implies that whenever Moon transits over these planets in Gochara, high possibilities of conflicts, disputes within the family & thereby impacts the peace of the native.

vi. Thus, the Avayogi Moon – though posited in the 11H – of gains will not support many gains. Also, it will only inflict Avayogam-bad luck, whenever it transits over the planets posited in its stars.

vii. 11H also signifies elder siblings. Because the Avayogi, is placed there in its own Avayogi star, neither the native nor the siblings will benefit from each other.

viii. If the Moon sign – Capricorn happens to be in Thithi Shunya (TS) – the affliction gets compounded. It is similar to that of a Bad man functioning – in an angry mood.

ix. The reason is – that the Mother gets her genetic Karma impacted, through the Native. Thus the Karmic impact gets genetically transmitted through & to one's progenies as well

x. **Thus, The Avayogi – even if posited in 11H of gains, will not deliver much gains**

xi. The Avayogi-Negative impact is well pronounced during its transit over S'ravana & during its MD/AD/PAD Dasha periods. Not much impact, in other planet dasha-bukti periods

xii. Further, the planets posited in the Avayogi star S'ravana only inflict full Avayogam. As regards the planet posited in Avayogi Moon's other 2 stars – Hasta, Rohini, the impact is only about 15% and that too may turn out to be an indirect benefit. The Dire malefic is only S'ravana – the Avayogi star – not others.

xiii. Similarly, any planet placed in the Yogi star of Pushya – will act as 100% yogi. In the instant case – its Jupiter. Any other planet placed in Saturn's other 2 stars (Anuradha, Uttrabhadrapada) will give marginal benefits (15%) only.

### B. Example 2

| | | | | | | |
|---|---|---|---|---|---|---|
| Lagna | | | | Lagna | | |
| | Natal | | | Saturn | Gochara | |
| | | Saturn-Hasta | | | | |

i. Here Saturn is in Hasta Nakshatra-Avayogi planets star in Natal chart. Now Saturn is in S'ravana – the Avayogi star in transit. This will inflict lot of troubles to the native as it's also Sadhe-sati.

ii. If the Native chooses to perform remedies-Parihara during the period of Hasta/S'ravana/Rohini Nakshatra days – it will only compound the miseries, no benefits at all. Similarly even temple visits during these periods will not help much.

iii. **Even the Yogi will fail to deliver – if placed in the Avayogi star or transits over them in Gochara.**

### C. Example: 3

| | | | | | | |
|---|---|---|---|---|---|---|
| | Natal Vishkumbha-Yoga | Jupiter | | | | Jupiter |
| | | Lagna | | Gochara | | |
| | | | | | | |

i. This Leo Lagna Native chart has exalted Jupiter in Pushya – the Yogi star. Accordingly, Jupiter is poised to give immense benefits wrt the positive gainful significations of 12H, like investment, gains from abroad etc. These benefits get compounded, when Jupiter transits in Cancer over Pushya Nakshatra.

i. **The Planet in Yogi star – even if posited in 12H of Vyaya Bhava will still choose to deliver the goodies of 12H**

ii. However, **Jupiter will deliver 100% benefit only when placed in the Yogi star of Pushya** – not much in other 2 stars of Saturn-the Yogi (only 15%)

## 2. Preeti Yoga

| Yogi Star | Yogi | Avayogi Star | Avayogi |
|---|---|---|---|
| Aslesha | Mercury | Dhanishta | Mars |
| **Preeti Characteristics** | | | |

Mercury (Aslesha) is the Yogi and Mars (Dhanishta) is the Avayogi.

➢ They do excel in white collar professions – requiring intelligence (Not much of Physical work – as Mars is the Avayogi).

➢ They should refrain from gaining anything from their siblings & exercise caution in property matters. It is good if they spend for their siblings

➢ They are courageous in general and are of loving nature

In General:

➢ This is an auspicious yoga – This is a good Muhurta for any Reconciliation and for Harmony and agreements between people & for public relations

➢ They are beautiful, of joyous and virtuous nature & are charitable too

➢ This promotes love marriages and good harmony with opposite sex

➢ They are lively, hardworking, and clever – achieve success in their life

➢ They are righteous, courageous, fortunate and balanced as well

➢ They have great communication skills, oratory and always love & feel happy by seeking happiness in others too

➢ They are selfless/unselfish and quite inquisitive

## Let us discuss few example charts

A.  Example: 1 – Chart for a Native born **in Preeti Yoga.**

| Mercury<br>Moon | | | Lagna |
|---|---|---|---|
| | Natal<br>Preeti Yoga | | |
| | | | |
| | | | |

i.  Lagna: Gemini, Moon in Pisces – Revati Nakshatra. Accordingly Mercury is the Yogi & Mars is the Avayogi. Running Dasha at Birth (MD) – Moon

ii.  At the outset, we may tend to feel that the Yogi planet Mercury, is in debility & hence not a benefic. However, it's in its own star-Revati, which cancels it debilitation effect to some extent.

iii.  Then a question may arise as to how the debilitation effect plays out?

iv.  The answer is that Mercury being the Yogi planet – will dole out all benefits specific to the native in abundance. However, it does cause harm to its Karakatwa signified relationships like younger sister, maternal uncle etc.

v.  Mercury, being a yogi – just protects the native from its evil effects directly/Mentally, despite its debilitation. The native will not feel/bother about these negatives.

B. **Example 2.**

| | | | |
|---|---|---|---|
| | Natal | | Mercury (Aslesha) |
| | Preeti Yoga | | |
| Lagna | | | |

i. This Sagittarius Asc native has his Yogi Mercury is in its own-Aslesha Nakshatra, hence bound to dole out full benefits. This, despite the 8H effects too in conjunction. The Native did get into lot of debts during his 8H Dasha, but also expanded his business in sync.

ii. He was in deep debt, throughout the Mercury MD – but also grew his business in tandem. He got Married, Progeny, Business growth, Status, Debts, all during this Mercury MD.

iii. **Yogi, delivered despite in Dustana, as it was posited in its own star.**

C. **Example 3.**

| | | | Lagna |
|---|---|---|---|
| | Natal | | |
| | | | |
| | | | Mercury |

i. The above Native born in Gemini Ascendant with AL (Asc Lord) Mercury in its other own sign of Virgo-but not in Preeti yoga.

ii. Mercury is not a Yogi for him. Though Mercury here is exalted& a benefic, it will deliver good results in general – but still less than the Debilitated Mercury (yogi) chart (Example 1) in comparison during its MD-AD.

iii. **This is because; Mercury-the yogi planet for Preeti Nama yoga – delivers more, despite its debility, than Non-Yogic exalted Mercury, in its Dasha periods in particular.**

D. **Example 4.**

| | | | Saturn |
|---|---|---|---|
| | Natal-Preeti Yoga | | Lagna |
| | | | Mercury |

i. The above Native born in Leo Ascendant with Mercury in its other own sign of Virgo & in Preeti yoga. Mercury is the Yogi for him. He also has Saturn in Aslesha-another star of Mercury.

ii. Saturn, despite being in a Dustana-inimical sign, will still deliver excellent results, as it is posited in the Yogi-Star Aslesha of Mercury. This Saturn inherits the benefic qualities of Yogi Mercury & delivers.

iii. **Thus we can infer that any planet, even if normally posited in weak dignity (viz.in Dustana/Debility) – if it's the Yogi or posited in a Yogi Star, turns out to a First Class Benefic. In Many cases, even better than an exalted – planet, which is not a Yogi.**

❖ ❖ ❖

## 3. Ayushman Yoga

| Yogi Star | Yogi | Avayogi Star | Avayogi | Remarks |
|---|---|---|---|---|
| Magha | Ketu | Shatabhisha | Rahu | |
| **Ayushman Characteristics** | | | | |

Ketu (Magha) is the Yogi and Rahu (Shatabhisha) is the Avayogi.

- They have a high karmic imprint, Long life & highly intuitive as Ketu (Magha) is the Yogi.
- Good at Finding faults and understanding defects. They are virtuous & law abiding in general and get good Progeny.
- May not be successful abroad & needs to be watchful before relocating/ travelling to foreign

In General:

- This confers a long life and Happiness of longer duration in comparison to others
- This is highly auspicious & Any work performed in this has a lasting effect
- They are avid travellers, Foodies and are target oriented in their profession and adhere to the rules
- They love music, Art & are wealthy in general
- They are leaders, respected by others & are endowed with a happy life. Well versed in judicial & policy matters of Govt
- They are healthy and are successful against enemies in any combat.

i. This is an Auspicious Yoga for long life. Even the Venerated Sage of Kanchi – Maha Periyava, had spoken highly of this yoga.

ii. The popular Ashirvad Terminology – "Ayushman Bhava" was coined, just to combine the blessing of both Bava Karana & Ayushman Yoga

iii. As the Nodes Ketu-Rahu are Yogi& Avayogi for this NamaYoga, regular Sarpa/Snake worship at Snake pits, facilitates fructification of promised Yogam

iv. However, they do encounter frequent problems from the Rahu signified Karaka Natives.

v. They also suffer/encounter frustrating experiences during Rahu-Ketu/Ketu-Rahu MD-AD Dasha periods. During these periods, they are either denied/unable to enjoy the benefits of the Yogas, normally promised in the chart.

## 4. Saubhagya Yoga

| Yogi Star | Yogi | Avayogi Star | Avayogi | Remarks |
|---|---|---|---|---|
| Purva Phalguni | Venus | Purvabhadrapada | Jupiter | |
| **Saubhagya Characteristics** | | | | |

Venus (Purva Phalguni in Leo) is the Yogi and Jupiter (Purva Bhadra) is the Avayogi

➢ The dad may do well financially after this Native's birth.

➢ Supports Venus related professions/business-like Fashion, Artifacts', fine arts etc.

➢ May be good in financial front too and live in comfort. They are devoted to God

➢ They may not get the right mentor or be the right guide to others. Though May be endowed with riches – need to be wary of others envy or curse – Should stick to the rules and be Dharmic to succeed.

➢ If afflicted may impact their children in progeny matters – May get to travel abroad

In General:

➢ This signifies Luck, good Fortune and Natives are amazingly fortunate.

➢ This is an Excellent Muhurta for Auspicious activities like Marriage, Grahapravesh, commencement of business etc.

➢ They Possess the gift of the gab and are very talkative & convincing – can easily influence others

> ➤ They are rich, knowledgeable, virtuous but a bit proud as well
> ➤ They do better outside their Native place
> ➤ They may possess some Special signs in their Body like Hands and feet etc. – implying good luck
> ➤ They do shine in Food industry
> ➤ They are attractive and in turn get attracted to the beautiful people of opposite sex as well

A. **Note:** The planet Venus is the Yogi and Jupiter is the Avayogi for this Nama Yoga. The Yogi star Purvaphalguni, is a Purna-Nakshtara (All Padas placed in a single sign), whereas the Avayogi star Purvabhadrapada is spread over 2 signs of the Zodiac. Thus we can infer

   i. Purvaphalguni Pada-1 Yogi is mapped on to Purvabhadrapada Pada-1 as Avayogi,

   ii. Purvaphalguni Pada-2 Yogi is mapped on to Purvabhadrapada Pada-2 as Avayogi,

   iii. Purvaphalguni Pada-3 Yogi is mapped on to Purvabhadrapada Pada-3 as Avayogi,

   iv. Purvaphalguni Pada-4 Yogi is mapped on to Purvabhadrapada Pada-4 as Avayogi.

B. Note: According to the above, we can summarise as follows

   i. For The Planet posited in Purvaphalguni Pada-1 – – The Planet posited in Purvabhadrapada Pada-1 is the Avayogi,

   ii. For The Planet posited in Purvaphalguni Pada-2 – – The Planet posited in Purvabhadrapada Pada-2 is the Avayogi,

iii. For The Planet posited in Purvaphalguni Pada-3 – – The Planet posited in Purvabhadrapada Pada-3 is the Avayogi,

iv. For The Planet posited in Purvaphalguni Pada-4 – – The Planet posited in Purvabhadrapada Pada-4 is the Avayogi & so on.

v. The variance is portrayed as under

| | | | | Jupiter | | | |
|---|---|---|---|---|---|---|---|
| Jupiter | Purvaphalguni-3 Purvabhadrapada-3 | | | | Purvaphalguni-4 Purvabhadrapada-4 | | |
| | | Venus | | | | Venus | |
| | | | | | | | |

C. General

i. Based on the degree of Yogi & Avayogi, there is a possibility that the planets placed, could form relationships, other than the normal 1-7, Sama saptama.

ii. The Native with this Saubhagya Yoga – may not get the fruits of its beneficence, if Jupiter& Venus in his natal chart are in close degrees by conjunction in the same sign or even in different signs (viz. Conjunct by degree only not by placement)

iii. Such a Yogi/Avayogi for Saubhagya viz. Venus-Guru, indicate the curse of a pregnant woman. However the effect is not so virulent (Mild only)

iv. Thus, even if they get to enjoy the material success – are deprived of the signified relationship or vice versa. They don't get both in tandem.

v. However, if Rahu+Mandhi are placed in Purvabhadrapada (Avayogi star) with no planet in Purvaphalguni (yogi star) in the Natal chart, Rahu-Jupiter MD-AD periods will let out a high karmic impact. This, in sync with the above curse of the pregnant woman – may prove fatalistic too in few cases.

## 5. Shobana Yoga

| Yogi Star | Yogi | Avayogi Star | Avayogi |
|---|---|---|---|
| Uttraphalguni | Sun | Uttrabhadrapada | Saturn |
| **Shobana Characteristics** | | | |

Sun (Uttra Phalguni) is the Yogi and Saturn (Uttra Bhadrapada) is the Avayogi

- ➢ May be endowed with a good ancestry – lineage and interest in Religion.
- ➢ May lead a Royal, Prestigious life. They have high self esteem
- ➢ They may not get to enjoy the Saturn related Significations – like having good workers – Servants etc. Also prone to serious ailments esp. of heart – kidney & need to be cautious even in small things

In General:

- ➢ This signifies art & beauty and is an auspicious yoga for any good work and travel
- ➢ They are very lucky in their profession and are good at anything which is artistic and tasteful!
- ➢ They are beautiful; get a beautiful spouse, virtuous and intellectuals with good IQ.
- ➢ They are good in public relations & impress others with their soft, gentle and intelligent conversation. They are a bit aggressive too occasionally!
- ➢ They get a good family and children and lead a satisfied life
- ➢ They are interested in Visual Art, Display and hence their home looks attractive

A. The planet Sun is the Yogi, and Saturn is the Avayogi for this Nama Yoga. The Yogi star Uttraphalguni is spread over 2 signs of the Zodiac (split Nakshatra), Whereas the Avayogi star Uttrabhadrapada is a Purna-Nakshtara (All Padas placed in a single sign). Thus we can infer

   i. Uttraphalguni Pada-1 Yogi is mapped on to Uttrabhadrapada Pada-1 as Avayogi,

   ii. Uttraphalguni Pada-2 Yogi is mapped on to Uttrabhadrapada Pada-2 as Avayogi,

   iii. Uttraphalguni Pada-3 Yogi is mapped on to Uttrabhadrapada Pada-3 as Avayogi,

   iv. Uttraphalguni Pada-4 Yogi is mapped on to Uttrabhadrapada Pada-4 as Avayogi.

B. Note: Please note that this implies the outcome as under.

   i. For The Planet posited in Uttraphalguni Pada-1 – – The Planet posited in Uttrabhadrapada Pada-1 is the Avayogi,

   ii. For The Planet posited in Uttraphalguni Pada-2 – – The Planet posited in Uttrabhadrapada Pada-2 is the Avayogi,

   iii. For The Planet posited in UttraphalguniPada-3 – – The Planet posited in Uttrabhadrapada Pada-3 is the Avayogi,

   iv. For The Planet posited in Uttraphalguni Pada-4 – – The Planet posited in UttrabhadraPada-4 is the Avayogi & so on

C. Few more Snippets on Shobana Yoga Natives.

   ✓ They often tend to lead a mechanical family life & that too, without any known cause/explicable reason

- ✓ They also feel something is lacking/inadequate/defective with everyone in the family
- ✓ Male Natives feel detached/disconnected from their father, but females after marriage, tend to feel that they are missing their father.
- ✓ The MD-AD, dasha-bukti periods of SUN-SAT & SAT-SUN are very challenging for them & they tend to miss out the benefits of many yogas promised in the chart
- ✓ They suffer from high Pitri-Dosha(forefathers curse) than others
- ✓ They also face issues from Ancestral properties/Inheritance like, even if they possess, may not get to enjoy the benefits

## 6. Athiganda Yoga

| Yogi Star | Yogi | Avayogi Star | Avayogi |
|---|---|---|---|
| Hasta | Moon | Revati | Mercury |
| **Athiganda Characteristics** | | | |

Moon (Hasta) is the Yogi and Mercury (Revati) is the Avayogi

- ➢ They do attain growth and fame in matters involving Intellectual qualities.
- ➢ Hasta is a cursed Star of Guru & hence May have difficulty in getting a progeny.
- ➢ But Many Famous personalities like Swami Vivekananda are born in this. They are adamant & of fighting nature.
- ➢ May indicate problem with the Mother

In General:

- ➢ This is among the most inauspicious yoga – not good for doing any work or travel – The results shall be harmful and dangerous

> This Native may not be compatible with his family and may bring dishonour/problems to them
> This Native could be arrogant, Quarrelsome and a hypocrite! Problematic to Mother & quick tempered too
> The Native born with this yoga – if has planets in Gandanta in his Natal chart – it's a double whammy – May resort to violent means of life. May also have problems in throat
> If well placed – May be courageous and benevolent too. But if driven to the tight corner – may shift the blame on others and escape
> They are detached but do relish quarrelling and fighting too
> They are strong willed and courageous and fairly honest too. They enjoy fine arts like movies, music etc.

A. Yogi & Avayogi point for Athiganda Yoga born native

|  |  |  |  |
|---|---|---|---|
|  |  |  | *Aslesha |
|  | Natal Yoga-Athiganda |  |  |
|  |  |  | *Hasta |

B. The above indicated Stars – Aslesha & Hasta play a crucial role in their life events. The planets posited in these 2 stars in the Natal chart & the planets transiting over these 2 stars in Gochara – determine the good-bad events promised in the native's life.

C. Example: 1 – Chart for a Native born in **AthigandaYoga.**

| Moon, Mer(R) | Lagna | | |
|---|---|---|---|
| | Natal AthigandaYoga | | |
| | | | |
| | | | |

i. Lagna: Aries, Yogi Moon in Pisces – Revati Nakshatra. Avayogi Mercury is retrograde in Pisces

ii. Yogi Moon Lords over 3 stars – Rohini (Taurus), Hasta (Virgo) & S'ravana (Cap) in that order. Similarly Avayogi Mercury lords over 3 stars – Aslesha (Can), Jyeshta (Sco), Revati (Pis) respectively

iii. The Yogi Moon is posited in the Avayogi star of Revati. Hence it keeps blocking the Avayogi from functioning in full capacity. While, this reduces the ill effect of the Avayogi – it also fritters away its good energy to deliver the goodies in that process

iv. **Thus if the Yogi is posited in the star of Avayogi – The Native is constrained to spend his energies/fortune for others – not for his own.**

v. The Native though amassed a good fortune during his good times – had to spend a lot for his family & to marry off his sisters, and remained help less when in need.

vi. However, if Yogi is in the star of Avayogi-it also has some positives. Like in this case, whenever he is down/depressed – if he gets a good book to read, he overcomes the gloom & gets refreshed.

vii. **The Yogi in order to overcome mental distress/mood – uses the Karakatwa signified by the Avayogi, like reading books (signifies Mercury). In that process – it depletes its capacity to deliver high benefits too.**

viii. In summation – the Net effect of this placement is – Yogi still delivers few goodies & also blocks the Avayogi from inflicting any misery.

ix. However, it is to be observed that, if the Avayogi Mercury had not been in retro, it would have immobilized the Yogi from delivering. **Thus, the Yogi posited in the star of Avayogi, who is in Retrograde, is fairly good.**

x. In the above case, the Yogi Moon is at 12H in Mercury's star. This signifies that the native spends a lot on hospitalization. Further, must spend on the Mercury signified relationships like younger sister, maternal uncle, younger son etc.

D. **Example 2:** Chart for a Native born in **AthigandaYoga.**

| | | | |
|---|---|---|---|
| Venus* | | | Lagna |
| | | | Saturn* |
| | Natal-Yoga Athiganda | | Moon<br>Mars |
| | | | |

*Venus in Revati 21°56' *Saturn in Aslesha

i. 5th Lord (5L) exalted in 10H-This Native held high positions in life – Good control over govt. But because the Avayogi – doubles up as Lagna Lord(LL), died under suspicious circumstances

ii. As Venus gets exalted in the Avayogi Star of Revati, he was caught in property-assets issues & was jailed too. The Native's leg too was severely afflicted when died.

iii. The Extreme success this native achieved turned counterproductive. Also the Karaka for Profession – Saturn is posited in the Avayogi star &which caused the death

iv. The Native had no planet in the Yogi Star & hence was unable to retain its fruits in the end.

E. **Example 3:** Chart for a Native born in **AthigandaYoga.**

| | | | |
|---|---|---|---|
| * | | | |
| Lagna | Natal | | Mars* |
| | Moon* | Mercury 1° | |

i. *Mars in Aslesha,*Moon in Jyeshta, *Revati in Pisces. Yogi Moon & its depositor Mars are in Parivartana (Exchange) but in Avayogi Stars

ii. Yogi is in debility in Avayogi star of Jyeshta, hence suffered on account of disputes with friends, Loss of reputation & legal actions-Jail etc. Also his leg affected when young

iii. The Position of Yogi in 10H & in Parivartana involving 6H&10H of Profession – His very success in profession turned out to be a curse – like separation from family, Friends & indulgence in vices.

iv. Also no planet in Yogi's star & hence was unable to retain/hold onto the success/benefits

v. He had nobody to rescue him out of trouble & left to fend for himself

vi. Also his Avayogi Mercury is placed in low degree in the **Bhadaka house** of his Lagna – Hence impacted relations with even good friends

vii. As the Avayogi Mercury lords 5H&8H – He is unable to get a progeny also and is under treatment.

viii. **In general, the Bhava-Lordship& Karakatwa of the Avayogi Mercury heaped untold miseries on this Native**

F. **Impactful Periods for this Native**

i. The Moon-Mercury and Mercury-Moon MD-AD periods are very impactful-Particularly through the planets transiting over the 6 yogi-Avayogi stars of Moon & Mercury.

ii. Especially, the planets placed/transiting in Hasta/ Revati stars will be very impactful – Life sustaining but also deprivation.

iii. The Native is forced to spend a lot of time-resources on the Bhava-Karaka (House) signified matters – relating to the Avayogi star

➢ Ex:If the Avayogi Star in 7H-For Marriage, in 5H-For Children, in 10H-Profession & so on

## 7.  Sukarma Yoga

| Yogi Star | Yogi | Avayogi Star | Avayogi |
|---|---|---|---|
| Chitra | Mars | Aswini | Ketu |
| **Sukarma Characteristics** | | | |
| Mars (Chitra) is the Yogi and Ketu (Aswini) is the Avayogi<br><br>➢ Benefits from siblings and (Spouse in case of female).<br>➢ Also gains through Property. They tend to like to accumulate good Punya, helpful but adamant too<br>➢ May be headless & hence lack clarity on many things.<br>➢ Not good advisers as they don't like to pursue/acquire knowledge outside their normal routine<br><br>In General:<br><br>➢ This is a good yoga especially to commence a new career, job and business<br>➢ They are generally wealthy, intelligent, of cheerful character, courageous with good Business Acumen<br>➢ They are dutiful, Dignified and disciplined in their performance. They are noble, charitable and their words and actions are in sync and harmony<br>➢ They are spiritual and caring and are of lovable character.<br>➢ They are very fortunate and Happy too | | | |

## Let us discuss few example charts

### A.  Example: 1 – Chart for a Native born in **Sukarma Yoga.**

| | | | Sun* |
|---|---|---|---|
| | | | |
| | Natal | | |
| | | | Lag/Mars |

Sun* – Mrigashira

i. Lagna: Virgo, Yogi Mars in Lagna Virgo – Chitra Nakshatra and in High degree (HD).

ii. Sun in 10H of Gemini in Dig Bala, in Mrigashira, that is another star of Mars-the yogi planet. Sun will be of immense benefit for this Native – Even in the periods of ganda viz.threats, money & wealth too will come in tandem.

iii. This Native is originally a smalltime Labourer, who joins a political party, participates in an agitation & gets jailed.

iv. After his release-was accorded all respect in the party and was nominated for elections. He won the elections & becomes a minister too. All happened in Yogi Mars in MD**.

v. The Yogi Mars, is also the ashtamesh-8L, but because in its own yogi star with Sun in Digbala – has given a ganda-trouble (jail) but also a great fortune too, in tandem. It may be noted that Mars lords 3H-8H for Virgo & hence imprisonment. Also Sun, the 12L because it's in Digbala & in Yogi Star – doled out a great yoga.

vi. Note: 3H-8H-12H are important for imprisonment. If it's by Avayogi-All the acts gets public, if Yogi-it's hidden from public scrutiny

**#Thus, the Yogi Mars after a ganda-suffering (in Jail), has afforded a great Vipareetha Raja yoga thereafter (Mantri).**

B. **Example: 2** – Chart for a Native born in Sukarma Yoga (5L in 5H but in Avayogi star)

|  | Mars |  | Ketu, Sat |
|---|---|---|---|
|  |  | Natal |  |
| Lag, Sun, Rahu |  |  |  |

i. Sun(9L) in Moola, Mars in Aswini, Rahu in Moola, Ketu in Mrigashira & Saturn in 7H in Digbala.

ii. Lagna: Sagittarius-a dual sign and Avayogi Ketu in 7H of Bhadaka sthan. Hence had more than one marriage

iii. Yogi Mars is the 5L in 5H but in the star of Avayogi – in Aswini. He did have good fame & status initially, and then stepped into the Avayogi MD of Ketu. He has **3 planets in Avayogi Ketu's star** & hence got into bad company/actions & loss of name and attendant insults as a consequence. Also, caused separation from family.

iv. He was almost beaten up by his own son & his 2nd Marriage at the old age – left an indelible black mark on his family. He got married when his son had grown up & to a woman with absolutely no compatibility to his family's cultural values – 100%Mismatch (Yogi Mars in 5H but in Avayogi Star)

v. **The most beneficial 5L (Mars) &9L (Sun) planets of this Lagna, despite in favorable houses-because of their placement in the Avayogi Star – inflicted this ignominy (apman).All these happened in Avayogi-Ketu MD.**

### C. #Impactful Periods for these Natives in General.

i. The Mars-Ketu and Ketu-Mars MD-AD periods are very impactful, particularly through the planets transiting over the 6 yogi-Avayogi stars of Mars & Ketu.

ii. Especially, the planets placed/transiting in Chitra/Aswini stars will be very impactful – Life sustaining but also deprivation.

iii. Mars is a first rate malefic for Virgo. Yet for those born in Sukarma Namayoga, Mars is bound to deliver benefits – **The yogi Mars is bound to deliver good even for an inimical ascendant born native, or at least restricts & inflicts less evil.**

iv. **Sukarma Yoga**, with Yogi Mars in its own Chitra Nakshatra – doles out immense good yoga-benefits to other Lagna Natives. However for Virgo Lagna, less evils & less goodies too

## 8. Dhriti Yoga

| Yogi Star | Yogi | Avayogi Star | Avayogi |
|---|---|---|---|
| Swati | Rahu | Bharani | Venus |
| **Dhriti Characteristics** | | | |
| Rahu (Swati) is the Yogi and Venus (Bharani) is Avayogi<br><br>➤ Hence any Rahu related profession like Technology/Modern Communication/Foreign etc. are supportive.<br>➤ They can lend on interest or act as commission agents too – have interest in others wealth<br>➤ They talk sweetly & are well qualified | | | |

> Need to be cautious in getting cheated-Possible losses in business and relationships.
> May not have stability in business or partnership s/Employment

In General:

> This Yoga is very auspicious for any construction activity like Bhoomi Pooja, Purchase of Land/House etc.
> They possess a Scientific/Analytical mind and are good in Science, Research and Space travel
> They are very patient & thoughtful – don't rush into any quick decision but are very decisive!
> They are fairly inclined towards opp. sex and look a bit restless and disturbed occasionally
> They are healthy, skillful, Successful and love to have good – peaceful, Routine family life

### A.  Impact in General.

i. Two Natives born under this yoga get married to each other – one born in Swati &the other in Bharani star. Their Marital life will be very sedentary-without much charm. The Yogas promised in their charts do not play out as promised.

ii. The mutual Compatibility takes a beating – viz. their desires are at tangent – when the Husband is in a good mood, the spouse will not be interested & vice versa

iii. If they have Rahu-Venus conjunction in their chart, Venus gets afflicted and causes more harm than Rahu. If their conjunction is close-it's more virulent-New Problems keep propping up, once the older ones are resolved.

    iv.  The Venus-Rahu and Rahu-Venus MD-AD periods are very impactful – Particularly through the planets transiting over the Swati Nakshatra of Rahu in Libra. Generally the MD-AD of Rahu-Venus& vice versa is troublesome.

    v.  Especially, the planets placed/transiting in Swati star will be very impactful – Transformative. Here, the Yogi star Swati is in the Avayogi house of Venus

**B.  Example**

| | | | | | | | |
|---|---|---|---|---|---|---|---|
| | Natal chart | | | | Transit – Gochara | | |
| | | Swati | | | | Rahu Venus(R) | |

    i.  Check the above proposition. A Dhriti yoga born Native with Avayogi Venus in Retrograde

    ii.  Venus(R) if conjunct with Rahu in any house for a Dhriti yoga native – inflicts great misery irrespective of Any Natal Lagna-Asc.

    iii.  This is particularly virulent – if this conjunction or transit takes place in Libra sign-Lorded by Avayogi-Venus

    iv.  Venus(R) Natives just keep repeating the same blunders very often, due to excessive desires-obsession.

## 9. Shoola Yoga

| Yogi Star | Yogi | Avayogi Star | Avayogi |
|---|---|---|---|
| Vishaka | Jupiter | Kritika | Sun |
| **Shoola Characteristics** | | | |

Jupiter (Vishaka) is the Yogi – Sun (Kritika) is the Avayogi

➢ Possess Profound knowledge of life/Occult and fairly honest and Dutiful.

➢ They are very Empathetic & Sympathetic to the suffering.

➢ Must refrain from being Egoistic, Argumentative and avoidable pride – This may play the spoil sport.

In General:

➢ This is not an auspicious yoga for Muhurta & any work undertaken/ completed in this yoga gives a sustained pain like a thorn in the flesh – A recurrent problem.

➢ They are Religious in Nature and are inclined to learn &do rituals like Havan & recitation of Mantras!

➢ They are Very intelligent, able and are proud too

➢ They are reliable & trust worthy, indulge in social service too.

➢ They are Spiritual but at the same time pursue Material comforts too – Good in wealth accumulation

➢ On the flip side – this also makes the Native Quarrelsome; suffer from diseases like Stomach/Rheumatic pains & possible Evil deeds too

➢ Despite fairly good and joyous moments in life – gives a tinge of unhappiness and disaffection too along with.

A. Let us discuss few example charts

| | | | |
|---|---|---|---|
| | | Shoola Natal | |
| *Uttrashada | | | |

i. These Natives have their Avayogi star of Uttrashada in their Yogi's sign of Sagittarius. Hence Sun-Jupiter & Jupiter-Sun MD-AD Dasha periods will be highly challenging. The planets posited/transiting over this Avayogi star, will dole out highly malefic outcomes

ii. The Natives born under this Shoola Yoga – with Sun& Jupiter (Avayogi-Yogi) conjunct in their natal chart are susceptible to fall in serious ailments – fatalistic too.

iii. Even though, this conjunction may start off as beneficial, will end up in disaster-in most cases. This is not a favorable conjunction – despite both being Atimitras (First rate friends)

B. **Example 1: Charts of Shoola Yoga Native with 2 children**

| | Sun (Kritika) | | |
|---|---|---|---|
| | Father | | |
| | | | |
| | | | |

| | | | | | |
|---|---|---|---|---|---|
| | 1st Child | | 2nd Child | | |
| | Uttraphalguni | | Vishaka | | |
| | | Moon | | Moon | |

i. This Native has Avayogi Sun exalted in Aries – but in its own star, Kritika. He begets two children – born in Uttraphalguni and Vishaka respectively.

ii. He says that, he suffered much after the birth of the first child. He never felt like pampering/loving that child. This despite that son being so helpful to him, he is unable to feel & appreciate his contribution. (All due to the birth in Avayogi star)

iii. On the other hand – he was always drawn to his daughter-2nd child born in Vishaka and appreciates her love and affection.

iv. In fact – he gave more to his daughter than his son while settling-apportioning his property/wealth – though, the elder son is not at fault at all.

v. **After all, it's the transmission of his own Karma – that gets delivered through the child born in the Avayogi star.**

vi. **As there are no other planets in, both Yogi-Avayogi stars – only the results of Aries (where sun is posited) got affected and not the Bhava of Suns lordship (5H-Leo).**

C. **Example 3: Charts of Shoola Yoga Native** (Avayogi Sun MD from 2007-13)

|  |  |  |  |
|---|---|---|---|
| Lagna |  |  | Rahu |
| Ketu | Natal |  |  |
| Mars | Sun, Mercury |  | Jupiter |

i. This Aquarius Ascendant Native has Avayogi – Sun Lord of 7th House (7L) in 10H of Scorpio in Digbala. She is well educated with no interest in employment-has a good spouse but no children

ii. This because the Avayogi Sun, is strongly placed – HD in 10H in Jyeshta star – with its Lord Mercury – Lord of 5H&8H too in conjunction. She is not inclined to adopt a child, even.

iii. However, she got excellent gains wrt the Bhavas aspected by the Yogi-Jupiter, viz. 12H/2H/4H, foreign settlement, Education, wealth& good family life, comforts & respect

iv. Had early marriage & tried hard for children (Medical treatments) during her 27-33 age under Sun MD – all without success. Finally declared as not fit to bear a child & hence subjected to distress.

v. **Thus the crucial MD-AD periods of a Planet, though in good Digbala – can't leave, without a lasting bitter experience – Because, it is the Avayogi for the Native**

## 10. Ganda Yoga

| Yogi Star | Yogi | Avayogi Star | Avayogi |
|---|---|---|---|
| Anuradha | Saturn | Rohini | Moon |
| **Ganda Characteristics** | | | |

Saturn (Anuradha) is the Yogi and Moon (Rohini) is the Avayogi

➢ Resorting to Shani Karaka professions are beneficial – like Housekeeping – cleaning, Oil – Iron & Health – Hospital related, Ambulance, Emergency workers etc.
➢ They should refrain from self-Pride
➢ May face possible problems from the family relations of the opposite sex.
➢ Also Possible black mark, suspicion in character – devoid of cleanliness.

In General:

➢ This is very inauspicious for commencement of any work – not a good Muhurta.
➢ Any work commenced gets into irreversible obstacles – waste of time, money and resources, Insurmountable arguments and fights.
➢ The Native born in this yoga get into many difficulties and leads a problematic life. They are often unhealthy too
➢ They may encounter bad – evil elements in the society & have to deal with them. But their perseverance & Determination may help them manage & come out of tight situations
➢ They are talkative & are inclined towards luxurious and a lavish life.
➢ They are angry, unhelpful and hard hearted

A. General

   i. The Avayogi Moon gets debilitated in Yogi Saturn's star of Anuradha, but gets exalted in Rohini-the Avayogi star.

   ii. This in effect indicates that Moon is a high malefic/ marginal benefic for this natives.

iii. This also signifies that the points, where the Yogis star in Avayogi's sign (Pushya in cancer) & Avayogi's star in Yogis sign (S'ravana in Cap), if gets related through planets in transit, (These stars are in 1-7) – portends very important life events of the native

B. Example: 1: **Charts of 2 Ganda Yoga Natives**

| | | | | | | |
|---|---|---|---|---|---|---|
| | A-Elder Brother – Anuradha | Lagna | | B-Younger Brother – Jyeshta | Lagna | |
| | Moon | | | Moon | | |

Here, both the Natives are born in Lagna-Leo, Scorpio-Moon, but in different stars. Here the Avayogi Moon, signifies multiple properties viz. Debilitated, Vyaya Bhava Lord (12L) in debility, in Yogis star & also in Digbala

i. The General interpretations are as under

ii. Debilitated Moon indicates – Less Merits and sickly dispensation

iii. Moon is 12L placed in 4H – implies long hospitalization

iv. Moon in Digbala-Implies either the Native or his Mother lives in Good dignity – viz. planet in Digbala in 4H-implies good house & vehicular comfort. Moon in debility there implies – comforts with mental worries/ tension

v. **Thus in summation – This implies that the Native despite in possession of all comforts – is still plagued by mental worries and tension.**

### C.  Chart A of Elder Brother:

i.  He is born in the Yogi star – Anuradha.

ii.  Though Moon gets debilitated here-but placed in the Yogic star – which cancels its debilitation (NBRY).

iii.  Even if he is wealthy – he will still receive immense blessings of his mother & may get furthermore wealth, gifted from her.

### D.  Chart B of Younger Brother:

i.  He is born in Jyeshta – not a Yogi star. Here too Moon gets debilitated – gets Digbala, but without cancellation of its debility. Because it is not backed by the Yogi star-not equipped to give a good yoga-benefit. Just doles out Digbala & Neecha impact

ii.  Hence, even if he receives goodies through his father, he will not receive any blessings/support of his mother. She may just part with, too little that too in reluctance. She may, just deliver it as a duty but not with happiness as done with the elder one.

iii.  **This is how we can differentiate the outcome of any planet placed in a Yogi star or placed otherwise.**

### E.  Example: 2 Chart of a Ganda Yoga Native

|  |  |  |  |
|---|---|---|---|
|  |  | Anuradha |  |
|  |  |  | Lagna, Saturn |
|  | Moon |  |  |

   i.   Leo Lagna, Moon in Scorpio-Anuradha, born in Ganda yoga. Saturn is the Yogi & is placed in Lagna itself.

  ii.   This Native is poised to multiply his Mothers assets exponentially. As the Yoga Lord is in Lagna-may make significant investments & grows further.

F.  **Example: 3** Chart of Ganda Yoga Native

| | | | |
|---|---|---|---|
| | Anuradha | | |
| | | | Lagna |
| | Moon | Saturn | |

   i.   Leo Lagna, Moon in Scorpio-Anuradha, born in Ganda yoga. Saturn is the Yogi & is exalted in Libra.

  ii.   Moon is in Digbala in 4H & in Yogi Star. This Native has received his share of Mothers assets, but allowed them to be used by his siblings and lives in good terms with them.

 iii.   It is to be noted that, he has not given up his assets/ shares but only the rights to use, to his siblings. This is just to ensure that he can focus on his growth more without diversion

G.  **Example: 4** Chart of Ganda Yoga Native

| | | | |
|---|---|---|---|
| Saturn | | | |
| | Anuradha | | |
| | | | Lagna |
| | Moon | | |

i. Leo Lagna, Moon in Scorpio-Anuradha, born in Ganda yoga. Saturn is the Yogi & is in Uttrabhadrapada star in Pisces.

ii. Though the Yogi Saturn is in the 8H from Lagna-it has doled out/will dole out good Yogas-Benefits to this native in the following periods Viz. During the MD of other planets but under the Saturn AD, when either of Sun/Moon/Saturn transits over the Star of the Yogi-Saturn.

## 11. Vriddhi Yoga

| Yogi Star | Yogi | Avayogi Star | Avayogi | Remarks |
|---|---|---|---|---|
| Jyeshta | Mercury | Mrigashira | Mars | |

**Vriddhi Characteristics**

Mercury (Jyeshta) is the Yogi and Mars (Mrigashira) is the Avayogi

➢ Hence may be naturally intelligent.
➢ May do well in the Medical field too as this sign favours Medical and Occult.
➢ They tend to be close & friendly to the Rich n powerful
➢ They need to be careful in property matters and Documents and with Siblings. Refrain from fights – violence and possible accidents

In General:

➢ This is very auspicious to commence any work – which will ensure incremental returns, growth and resultant Happiness
➢ These Natives are endowed with excellent personality traits, good physique, Attitude etc. – which also gets imbibed by their spouse and children
➢ Their childhood environment shapes up their personality and progress. They are family oriented and love, care and value their spouse and children

> They are analytical, kind hearted, intelligent and love Nature and of loving nature.
> They are endowed with good intelligence, stature and authority and therefore accumulate wealth, name and fame – Make significant progress in their business

### A. **General**

   i. The planet Mercury is the Yogi and Mars is the Avayogi for this Nama Yoga.

   ii. The Yogi star Jyeshta is a Purna-Nakshtara (All Padas placed in a single sign), whereas the Avayogi star Mrigashira is spread over 2 signs of the Zodiac (split star) – Thus it deprives the fruits of Yogi-if placed in its Gemini Sign portion more.

### B. Example: 1 – Chart for a Native born **in Vriddhi Yoga.**

|  |  |  | Mars |
|---|---|---|---|
|  |  |  |  |
|  |  |  |  |
|  | Lagna |  |  |

   i. Lagna Scorpio in Jyeshta star.

   ii. The LL Mars-the Avayogi if in his own star Mrigashira may inflict some physical deficiency or a permanent ailment.

C.  Example: 2 – Chart for a Native born **in Vriddhi Yoga.**

|  |  |  |  |
|---|---|---|---|
|  | Natal – Vriddhi |  |  |
|  | Moon<br>Mercury |  | Mars |

i.  Moon & Mercury posited in Yogi star-Jyeshta and Mars in Chitra star. This is a case of Nakshatra Lord (NL)/ Star lord being, the Yogi and Sign Lord (Rashi Lord) being, the Avayogi. Also Mrigashira in Gemini & Chitra in Virgo – both are Avayogi Mars's stars.

ii.  This indicates an incompatibility between Thought& Action. They are at tangent.

iii.  The Yogi Mercury is in Yogi star-Promises great yoga-benefits.

iv.  There is also a Nakshatra Parivartana between the Yogi & Avayogi. This implies he gets rewarded/Money from an unexpected quarters – not from a planned source-activity.

v.  If the Nakshatra Lord (NL) is the Yogi and the Rashi – Sign Lord is the Avayogi-the native may change his course/target all of a sudden.

vi.  Nakshatra is an internal organ & Rashi (sign) is external organ – Here Scorpio indicates the organ below waist (reproductive, uterus, bladder, bowel etc.). Each internal organ represents a Nakshatra.

vii.  In the above case – the dispositer/sign owner of Yogi-Mercury is the Avayogi-Mars. If this native gets some affliction in the nerves (Mercury), it may not be immediately visible outside – but only after the infection becomes virulent

viii. **# If the Nakshtara-Starlord is the Yogi and Sign lord is the Avayogi – The Healing process does not work easily – even if it's by an expert.**

## 12. Dhruva Yoga

| Yogi Star | Yogi | Avayogi Star | Avayogi |
|---|---|---|---|
| Moola | Ketu | Ardra | Rahu |

| **Dhruva Characteristics** |
|---|
| Ketu (Moola) is the Yogi and Rahu (Ardhra) is the Avayogi<br><br>➢ They are Society conscious and also are family oriented.<br>➢ May deviate from tradition too.<br>➢ They respect Elders & keep up their promises and are Patient too.<br>➢ They are Prone to Karmic diseases of Skin, poisoning and blood impurities – Delay in Marriage and Self pride<br><br>In General:<br><br>➢ This is lucky for Construction of a House or any other activity related to Home-But not for purchase of Vehicles.<br>➢ These Natives have robust health, mental peace and patience and therefore remain much focused in life<br>➢ They have the blessings of Knowledge & Wealth, Trust worthiness & thereby command love and respect from Society<br>➢ They have high intellectual qualities but are also drawn towards possible Evil deeds & Acts which may create secret enemies and possible obstacles in their endeavours |

*Note: The Dhruva Yoga born natives should not marry those born in Ardra Nakshatra, if both are in the same yoga. However if the other one is born in a different yoga-it's okay

A. **Example: 1 – Chart for a Native born in Dhruva Yoga.**

| | | | Lagna |
|---|---|---|---|
| | Natal-Dhruva | | |
| Moon | | | |

i. Gemini Asc with Lagna in Ardra & Moon in Moola star and born in Dhruva NamaYoga. Lagna &Moon are in Samasaptama (1-7)

ii. This Native is working in abroad &longs to return to the Native India. However, after landing here, he will again start thinking of going back.

iii. **# Thus, he is not able to enjoy what he wants, even if he gets that, by choice. This is the impact of Yogi-Avayogi if in Samasaptama (1-7 placements).**

iv. **#Tips:**

  ✓ **In** Match making, we must ensure that the distance between Sun & Venus is not very high. Also in D9-Mercury is not in 1-3-7-11.

  ✓ Natives with Ketu as the Yogi planet – gets good Yogam irrespective it's placed Bhava. Those who take loans and build houses, do business are well supported by Ketu. The Natives who progressed through loans – mostly have Ketu as yogi.

  ✓ The Natives with Ketu as yogi – if get employed in temples – The temple gets developed easily.

❖ ❖ ❖

## 13. Vyaghata Yoga

| Yogi Star | Yogi | Avayogi Star | Avayogi |
|---|---|---|---|
| Purvashada | Venus | Punarvasu | Jupiter |
| **Vyaghata Characteristics** | | | |

Venus (Purvashada) is the Yogi Jupiter (Punarvasu) is the Avayogi

- Good prosperity and Happiness in the family after childbirth & wealthy too.
- They may inherit good wealth from dad's ancestry
- May be subjected to fake allegations & Documentations etc. get punished for no fault.
- Hence should exercise utmost caution and stick to the rules & be honest. They have an unpredictable behavior too.

In General:

- This Yoga is not supportive/unlucky for undertaking any work – it's highly negative and may hit the block anytime. Better to avoid this for Muhurta
- They are good at Multitasking & are highly skilled and versatile. Hence may be famous and appreciated by others & fairly successful too
- They are bit eccentric and have an angry temperament – Hence their colleagues/subordinates may not feel free to talk to them
- They are Egoistic, Aggressive and hence may accumulate many adversaries too, despite their versatility
- In general they are cruel hearted, violent and abusive and are unpopular
- They have some prominent but peculiar eyes

A. The natives born in Vyaghata – will have their life impact mainly through the planets placed in **Vishaka** (The Avayogi planet (JU) star in Yogi's (VE) house) and in **Purvashada** (The Yogi's star in the Avayogi's house) as marked under

B.  Example

| | | | |
|---|---|---|---|
| | | | |
| | Natal-Vyaghata | | |
| *Purvashada | | *Vishaka | |

i.  **Purvashada & Vishaka are pointers signifying a pregnant woman's curse.** Venus signifies pregnant women & Jupiter signifies Root-Maker

ii.  In a Prashna Kundli, if we come across Vyaghata Nama yoga – we can straight away infer that there is a Stree – Shraap of a pregnant woman/a curse from a woman who desired to lead a happy life with child.

iii.  Also Jupiter-Venus conjunction indicates such a curse.

iv.  Hence these Natives are advised to beget children – during the MD-AD periods not relating to Jupiter and Venus. Check, mainly the AD-which is more powerful than MD.

## 14. Harshana Yoga

| Yogi Star | Yogi | Avayogi Star | Avayogi |
|---|---|---|---|
| Uttrashada | Sun | Pushya | Saturn |
| **Harshana Characteristics** | | | |
| Sun (Uttrashada) is the Yogi and Saturn (Pushya) is the Avayogi<br><br>➢ Indirect benefit from Govt – Quasi Govt related (Capricorn). They are Intelligent, honest and popular.<br>➢ Encounter possible problems from subordinates and workers. | | | |

> Possible karmic imprint from untimely death from mother's side (as it is in Cancer)

In General:

> This is very auspicious yoga and is a Harbinger of happiness and prosperity in the life of a person
> They are born leaders and their inherent leadership comes to the fore based on the opportunities & life challenges
> They are fortunate, Scholarly and highly meritorious, Experts in Traditional knowledge – Sastras. Hence command high respect in the society
> They are highly focused, creative, authoritative & hence very Dynamic and dominant too. They are high achievers in the field of creative art and literature & easily overcome opposition.
> They have a very tender body, liking for ornaments & a flair for occult Vidhya.

A. General

    i. The natives born in **Harshana** – will have their life impact, mainly through the planets placed in **Uttrashada** (The Yogi's star in the Avayogi's house-sign) as marked under

|  |  |  |  |
|---|---|---|---|
| *Uttrashada | Natal-Harshana |  |  |
|  |  |  |  |

    ii. The natives born in Harshana – if have their Lagna/ Ascendant in Avayogi Saturn's stars or in Yogi Sun's star, any planet posited in/transiting over the Uttrashada, will dole out their respective Avayogi-Yogi attributes.

    iii. Also if the MD-AD – PAD lords are in Uttrashada, the results will be impactful.

B.  Example: 2 – Chart for a Native born in **Harshana Yoga.**

| | | | |
|---|---|---|---|
| | Natal-Harshana | | |
| Sun, Sat | | | Lagna |
| | | | |

The above Native has Yogi-Avayogi Sun & Saturn conjunct in Yogi's star. They may have differences with their Son(s) but may not fight much. Because Sun is the Yogi – Father will give in & Saturn is the Avayogi – Son will always be raring to fight.

i.   This Sun-Saturn Conjunction also indicates issues in the mobility of Sperms. Hence for treatment of fertility/Bone problems, MUHURTA in this Nama yoga needs to be avoided.

C.  Example: 3 – Chart for a Native born in **Harshana Yoga.**

Natal-Harshana:

| | | | Lagna |
|---|---|---|---|
| | | | |
| Sun, Sat | Natal-Harshana | | |
| | | | |

Transit-Accident day:

| | | | Lagna |
|---|---|---|---|
| | | | Sun |
| | Saturn | Transit-Accident day | |
| | | Moon | |

i.   This Gemini Native has this Yogi-Avayogi conjunct in Cap. As they hold lordships of 3H&8H, he got involved in an accident during Sun-Saturn, MD-AD period. As Sun is the Yogi – even though it was a major accident, he recovered soon with minor issues.

ii. At the time of Accident Saturn was transiting in 8H in Yogis star, Moon in Anuradha & Sun in Pushya (Avayogi stars)

## 15. Vajra Yoga

| Yogi Star | Yogi | Avayogi Star | Avayogi | Remarks |
|---|---|---|---|---|
| S'ravana | Moon | Aslesha | Mercury | |
| **Vajra Characteristics** | | | | |

Moon (S'ravana) is the Yogi and Mercury (Aslesha) is the Avayogi,

➤ This comes with the Responsibility towards Family.
➤ In general – Obedient, Calm & Collected in behavior and Interested in Agriculture & Farming etc.
➤ Victorious against enemies but inclined towards certain negative traits too
➤ Subject to Serious health issues relating to Bowels & Kidney etc. Females may have possible Uterus problems

In General:

➤ This yoga is not auspicious for purchase of Vehicles, clothes or ornaments. Susceptible for Accidents
➤ These Natives are very Strong, courageous and have immense physical strength and stamina – and therefore are designed for jobs calling for good physical activity – including wars & weapons
➤ They are analytical & fault finders. Hence prone to be labeled as troublesome guys. They are fit for Audit; Superintendent works if they channelize their skills productively
➤ They are helpful and caring for the underprivileged and are charitable too
➤ They are wealthy & respected in society in general. They are intelligent but have a sharp tongue & speak the truth. They love to wear good Jewelry/ornaments and have expertise in this domain too (To identify fake jewelry etc.)
➤ If afflicted may indulge in shady activities too.

A.  General

i.  The natives born in Vajra yoga are very practical-Pragmatic in nature. But the Avayogi Mercury does not leave them to live in line with their pragmatic approach.

ii.  They take lead in taking care of their younger sister's needs; conduct all their welfare events like Marriage etc.-Yet not of much use/reciprocation. They will have to let go with a broad mind.

iii.  They tend to get worried about their head and legs.

iv.  **The Capricorn Lagna born natives – have Avayogi Mercury as 6L&9L.Hence their prayers are not easily answered (9L is Avayogi).**

v.  They are also prone to get involved in disputes, if they take loans etc. Both 6H & 9H tend to be inimical to them like they don't get along with their bosses & father.

vi.  **<u>Generally if the Trinal lords 5L/9L happen to be the Avayogi – Life itself is a dispute/struggle to the extent of 70%</u>**

B.  Example: 2 – Chart for a Native born in **Vajra Yoga.**

|  |  |  |  |
|---|---|---|---|
|  |  |  |  |
| Lagna | Natal-Vajra | | |
| Moon |  |  |  |

i.  Lagna (Asc) is in Yogi Star of S'ravana &Yogi Moon in Sagittarius. Moon in 12H supports great income when relocated to outside state/country-

ii.  Moon in 12H signifies losses in own business & but supports income from relocation to Abroad-Other states.

iii.  Moon as Yogi promises good income, name & fame at places outside the nativity. This however inhibits living in a joint family

## 16. Siddhi Yoga

| Yogi Star | Yogi | Avayogi Star | Avayogi |
|-----------|------|--------------|---------|
| Dhanishta | Mars | Magha | Ketu |
| **Siddhi Characteristics** | | | |

Mars (Dhanishta) is the Yogi and Ketu in Magha is the Avayogi

- They are Calm, Composed and thoughtful behavior
- Strong personality traits, Leadership and Endowed with Land and Riches.
- Honour their commitments to others. They tend to be good to everyone and are avid tourists
- They may not be in direct employment/Govt.
- Also Could be unlawful or don't do justice to what they are supposed to (Affliction of Ketu's positive traits)

In General:

- This Yoga implies Accomplishment & any work done during this yoga promises good success – Hence a lucky and auspicious one
- They are strong – both physically & mentally and therefore are proficient in any job. They perform any job with equal finesse
- They are intelligent and endowed with all desired prosperity incl. children – A happy life in general
- They are charitable and compassionate and help the poor
- They are very skillful, focused and hence achieve high Material success
- On the flip side, may cause some deep health problems too. We can see highly evolved saints – encountering serious health afflictions in their pursuit after siddhi
- They are very liberal, sweet and satvik and are good at scriptures and Adhyatmik Knowledge – of Brahman etc.

A. Siddhi Namayoga Natives – though face problems if Sun-Mars are conjunct in their natal chart in any house, the problems get multiplied if this conjunction happens in Leo-Magha Nakshatra.

B. Example: 1 – Chart for a Native born in **Siddhi Yoga.**

|  |  |  |  |
|---|---|---|---|
|  |  |  |  |
| Lagna | Natal-Siddhi yoga |  | Sun<br>Mars |
|  |  |  |  |

i. Sun& Mars conjunct in Magha (Leo) – This Native got married during Mars MD. The spouse died of Heart attack on the 9th day of marriage.

ii. Mars as 11L supported the Marriage – but its placement in 8H & in Avayogi star caused this calamity.

C. Example: 2 – Chart for a Native born in **Siddhi Yoga.**

|  |  |  |  |
|---|---|---|---|
|  |  |  |  |
|  | Natal-Siddha yoga |  | Sun<br>Mars |
| Jupiter<br>Moon |  | Lagna |  |

i. Libra Asc, Sun-Mars conjunct in 11H and Moon & Jupiter in star – Moola (sag)

ii.   This Native suffers from frequent Fits-seizures. The reason-the Karaka planets for the head, Sun& Mars posited in the Avayogi Ketu's star.

iii.  It is to be noted that this conjunction, does receive the aspect of Jupiter-but this aspect is from the **Jupiter posited in Avayogi star**. Jupiter also happens to be the 6L. This has just extended his longevity – but no relief/cure from the ailment

iv.   Further, Moon is the Lord of 10H-karmasthan, which is also posited in Avayogi's star. Hence this Native suffered from the paralysis (hand-leg) right from his birth.

# 17. Vyatipata Yoga

| Yogi Star | Yogi | Avayogi Star | Avayogi |
|---|---|---|---|
| Shatabhisha | Rahu | Purvaphalguni | Venus |
| **Vyatipata Characteristics** | | | |

Rahu (Shatabhisha) is the Yogi and Venus (Purva Phalguni) is the Avayogi

➤ Inherit high karmic backlogs from forefather's ancestry & pass on to their progeny too

➤ May Dole out a good Material Yoga but spoils relationship related Significations.

➤ Inclined to neutralize the enemies but suffer much in life and not so good in education.

➤ Possible afflictions through diseases of Body, mind and from opposite sex

In General:

➤ This is an inauspicious yoga for Muhurta – Any new work commenced in this Yoga may lead to heavy losses, Arguments with partner etc. Hence should be avoided mostly

> These Natives have a challenging childhood – Hurdles, Problems and failures are the norms
> These challenges help them get moulded as a tough individual with determination – thereby slowly achieve success from their youth & thereafter.
> This however can make them hard hearted and cruel, unstable & Rigid and obstruct others efforts.
> They are argumentative and non-conformists – However they do obey their parents
> They are lavish and extravagant in spending & are late achievers

## A. General

i. These Vyatipata natives are prone to get into bad habits, easily.

ii. As Venus is the Avayogi, it's the reason for many of these natives leading a life away from home & in anonymity – in possible confinements too.

iii. These effects may play out only during Rahu-Venus, Venus-Rahu sub periods, not always. No need to fear if they don't face Venus MD during their prime age.

iv. Natives having Venus as the Avayogi should not run after, in search of sudden Dhana yogas like lottery, shares etc. & lose their existing wealth in such speculations.

v. Males get troubled by Females & Females by other females. Many lose their peace by a competitive attitude &envy.

vi. They are prone to Venus signified diseases like Skin Pigmentation, Kidney ailments, Venereal diseases etc. – not easy to seek cure & which causes a dent in public image.

B. Example: 1 – Chart for a Native born in **Vyatipata Yoga.**

| | | Venus | |
|---|---|---|---|
| Lagna | | | |
| | Natal-Vyatipata | | |
| Moon | | | |

i. Lagna in Yogi Nakshatra in Aquarius, Moon in Sagittarius – Avayogi Venus in Taurus

ii. This Native is a businessman dealing with export of garments-invested heavily, based on the assurance of a female associate.it was going well, but all of a sudden the female died in an accident & the native had to expend a lot on that female &the garments got wasted and sold as scrap for a song. He got into a big debt trap & unable to come out of it.

iii. #Note: The female did not trouble or cheat – it's just that the native made an ambitious investment based on the advice of a female – Avayogi Venus effect played out.

## 18. Variyan Yoga

| Yogi Star | Yogi | Avayogi Star | Avayogi | Remarks |
|---|---|---|---|---|
| Purvabhadrapada | Jupiter | Uttraphalguni | Sun | |
| **Variyan Characteristics** | | | | |

Jupiter (Purva Bhadrapada) is the Yogi and Sun (Uttra Phalguni) is the Avayogi

- Mostly Stay outside their Native (this star extends to Pisces – Air to water).
- They are Prone to problems from Bosses, opponents and Dad too.
- They are Skilled in Camouflaging the Truth.
- Helpful to relatives and they get a good spouse.
- May be subject to problems from the powers that are.
- Must exercise caution in taking loans on high interest and refrain from avoidable disputes and self-Pride.

In General:

- This Yoga is Auspicious to commence any kind of work – Fairly positive
- They are very strong, confident, and powerful and focused – Highly goal oriented and rest only after attainment. Even enemies hold them in awe!
- They are highly creative characters and are proficient in Music, Dance and similar art forms. If they focus their career in these – Quick success guaranteed. They have an innate ability and natural urge in these fields
- They are also inclined in Religion & philosophy & Occult Vidhya
- They have an impressive persona and make everyone around happy and also acknowledge their wealth of knowledge & skills.
- Even their spouses are proud of them
- In short, they are humble, virtuous, and generous in spending & are sensual too – they induce positivity in others. Creative talent is their forte

A. General

    i. If the Putrakaraka/Sun gets posited in the Avayogi star of Uttraphalguni-it affects Putra Bhagya-Progeny

ii.  Natives born in any Lagna, but in Variyan Namayoga, if afflicted by Cancer-gets cured easily – Their cells get renewed, regenerated faster. **This is a gift – Specific to this yoga**.

iii.  This yogi star Purvabhadrapada is a split star – 3pada in Aquarius and the 4th in Pisces. Because its Saturn's house – it conceals the diseases from getting into open.

iv.  They are vulnerable to Karmic-Ailments like Depression, Pains, stunted mental growth, Liver issues and even their demise causes pain in others. This Yoga causes serious physical ailments, genetic disorders & possible dent in fertility.

v.  They are highly devotional too.

vi.  One **Variyan** Native had undertaken the remedy of carrying Milk pot to Lord Muruga temple for years, on Uttraphalguni (Avayogi star) days, but without results. He was advised to do this in Pushya-he came back after 2 years & confirmed that his problems in property, cash, all got resolved.

vii.  **# This is the Karma effect – the Native gets misdirected without understanding the reasons. This yoga is highly karmic.**

# 19. Parigha Yoga

| Yogi Star | Yogi | Avayogi Star | Avayogi | Remarks |
|---|---|---|---|---|
| Uttrabhadrapada | Saturn | Hasta | Moon | |
| **Parigha Characteristics** | | | | |

Saturn (Uttra Bhadrapada) is the Yogi – Moon (Hasta) is the Avayogi

➢ Good for Water related profession (Pisces impact). Frequent fliers and indulge in water – Might drink.

➢ They are skilled in deception, Critical and may not be rich

➢ They are Prone to karmic ailments – infections, Diseases of Skin. Possible Progeny issues.

In General:

➢ This Yoga is generally inauspicious for any activity – except for plotting and working against an enemy. Not for any positive work

➢ These Natives have multifaceted skills and are masters of many subjects. Hence they are famous & win many accolades

➢ They are born fighters and have interests in Arms & Ammunition related gadgets.

➢ However this fighting nature needs to be kept under check right from their childhood so that they don't harm others

➢ They are fond of travelling & explore many places. They are soft spoken, not so hungry & are endowed with a family life

➢ They do help out many from Court cases – imprisonment by hook or crook – like false representation etc. & defeat their enemies

## A.  General

i.  This Yogi-Avayogi combine is in a Punarbhu-Dosha type setup for this Parigha yoga Natives (Also for Vishkumbha & Ganda).These Natives should desist from performing remedies on Mondays. They can do them on Saturday instead – for better results.

ii. **Let us discuss an identical Birth chart – but born in different Nama yogas. This modifies the chart like – the speed of delivery of planetary results & decision making capacity of the native etc.**

B. Example: 1 – Chart for a Native born in **Parigha Yoga.**

| | | | |
|---|---|---|---|
| SAT JUPITER | | | |
| | Parigha Namayoga | | |
| | | | MOON |

✓ Yogi Saturn in Pisces (Uttrabhadrapada) &Avayogi Moon in Hasta (Virgo).**Yogi-Avayogi are in Samasaptama (1-7) and hence the Native will be of Procrastinating type-delays his decisions**

C. Example: 2 – Similar chart but born in Shoola Namayoga

| | | | |
|---|---|---|---|
| SAT JUPITER | | | |
| | **Shoola Namayoga** | | |
| | | | MOON |

i. This native born in Shoola Yoga – for him Saturn & Moon are not Yogi/Avayogi. But Jupiter is a yogi & in own sign. This Native during the concerned MD-AD of Saturn-Moon will decide & act fast, without delays. This Punarbhu Dosh (with Saturn-Moon in 1-7 but with Jupiter) signifies an Achiever – Born to Achieve.

ii.  Thus, the Natal chart of the above 2 natives – though with similar placements dole out differential outcome – because they are born under different Nama Yoga.

## 20. Shiva Yoga

| Yogi Star | Yogi | Avayogi Star | Avayogi |
|---|---|---|---|
| Revati | Mercury | Chitra | Mars |
| **Shiva Characteristics** | | | |

Mercury (Revati) is the Yogi and Mars (Chitra) is the Avayogi

➤ Good re'earchers and Creative inventors – Intelligence in Para Vidhya – Higher Matters
➤ Good caretakers of parents and friends. Generally Happy and prosperous too.
➤ They are Susceptible to Impurities in Blood and Blood related problems, thalassemia etc.

In General:

➤ This Yoga has connection with Lord Shiva and hence Auspicious and beneficial. Any work commenced in this yoga promises Success
➤ They are highly benevolent, Spiritual, Traditional and are reasonably evolved human beings
➤ They have the blessings of Lord Shiva, knowledge of Scriptures/Vedic Hymns and control of senses – desires
➤ They always focus in solving other's Problems & dedicate themselves in the services of society with a clean heart& devotion
➤ They are beautiful, fortunate, Satvik, Cool and Matured
➤ They are contented and never display their wealth though others acknowledge them
➤ They are poised towards realisation of higher self

A. **General**

   i. Note: If Mercury & Mars are conjunct in the Natal chart of the Natives born in Shiva Namayoga – It gives good intelligence & success in Education. At the same time – they tend to fall in love at the student age itself esp. during their MD-AD. They however, get to fall in love with wrong persons-not so compatible, which affects their life.

   ii. Those Shiva Natives, who are in Engineering, need right mentors to succeed.

   iii. The Planets placed in Yogi Mercury & Avayogi Mars-connected Rashi-Nakshatra & transits over these – play significant role in the life events of the Native

   iv. **Even if one of these planets in retrograde-the impact is stronger. Retro's just delay, don't deny.**

B. Example: 1 – Observe the Rashis indicated by Numbers 1,2,3,4 in the Chart

| 1 Pis | | | 2 Gem |
|---|---|---|---|
| | | | |
| | | | |
| 4 Sco | | | 3 Vir |

   i. The Yogi-Avayogi Conjunction of Mercury – Mars, if happens in their stars Revati (Pis) &Chitra (Virgo) respectively-Promises important life events during their MD-AD & Transits

   ii. Similarly, if this happens in their stars Mrigashira (Gem) &Jyeshta (Sco) respectively-also Promises important life events, during their MD-AD & transits

iii. Even though Mercury is in debility in Revati in Pisces – it delivers excellent results for Shiva Namayoga Natives – because it's the Yogi. It becomes stronger, if in retro & strengthens other retro planets too in its sign. No other planet can prevent/divert the feeling of love, infused by Mercury.

iv. **The Thumb rule is Mercury gains strength when in retrograde & also strengthens other retro planets posited in its sign**

C. Example: 2 – Chart for a Native born in **Shiva Namayoga.**

| | | | |
|---|---|---|---|
| Mercury | | | |
| | Shiva Namayoga | | |
| | | | Lagna, Mars |

i. Lagna: Virgo, Avayogi – Mars in Virgo – in Chitra Nakshatra. Yogi Mercury in Pisces – in Revati Nakshatra. Accordingly, Saturn is the Yogi & Moon is the Avayogi. Running Dasha at Birth (MD) – Moon

ii. Though, Mercury is debilitated in Pisces, because it is in Yogi Nakshatra of Revati-doles out immense benefits (300%)

iii. The planet Mars is the Avayogi & is also the Lord of 3H&8H-dire malefic (400%)

iv. During the AD periods of Mercury under the MD periods of other planets, the native will raise in his position/status. On the other hand, the AD periods of Mars under the MD of other planets – signifies a fall in position.

v. As the lagna lord Mercury is Neecha in 7H – it signifies few self-inflicted miseries & lower acts also. As a Yogi- it is bound to give good results for his activities too.

vi. **Lagna Lord signifies – Physical Body & Life and Yogi- signifies the good acts of the Native**

vii. **Note:**

- ✓ For Virgo Lagna, Mars lords the 8$^{th}$ house & hence bound to give pains-insults. If it's the yogi for Virgo – it will truncate the benefits-goodies and also minimize the pains. If Mars is the Avayogi for Virgo Asc, the Pain-disgrace gets multiplied
- ✓ The MD-AD-PAD periods associated with both Yogi-Avayogi breeds disappointments in abundance – even the Times turn inimical.

viii. Example: Research purposes

1. 15/06/1996 at 21.20 – Shoola Yoga and
2. 10/07/1996 at 21.20 – Shoola Yoga

- ✓ Let us observe the actual difference between the effects of these Namayoga.
- ✓ In the first case (1) above – Sun was posited at 61°.00 and Moon at 56°.32. The distance between them is just <5°.
- ✓ In the Second case (2) above – Sun was posited at 84°.51 and Moon at 29°.03. The distance between them is 55°.

ix. Hence Sun & Moon are at a different distance and in different Rashis under the same yoga. This quantum of impact of Yogi/Avayogi too gets modified in accordance with this

❖ ❖ ❖

## 21. Siddha Yoga

| Yogi Star | Yogi | Avayogi Star | Avayogi |
|-----------|------|--------------|---------|
| Aswini | Ketu | Swati | Rahu |
| **Siddha Characteristics** | | | |
| Ketu (Aswini) is the Yogi and Rahu (Swati) is the Avayogi<br><br>➢ Highly Creative & are Capable of Creating anything for themselves like Land/kingdom etc.<br>➢ Good in gaining wealth, power and contented<br>➢ Possible Obstacles in all facets of progress in life like Job/Marriage/ progeny if afflicted<br><br>In General:<br><br>➢ This is an auspicious yoga and any work done in this gives good outcome<br>➢ These Natives are Truthful, Control their Senses and are inclined to possess profound knowledge on Science and Philosophy<br>➢ They have a strong inclination to acquire and perform Mantra/Tantra related activities to attain their objectives. They perform such a Sadhana & Worship the related God to achieve this<br>➢ They are good legal & relationship consultants and are spiritual.<br>➢ They are endowed with an attractive and smart spouse, adequate wealth, and comforts.<br>➢ They are efficient, high achievers & accomplish Multiple tasks by their Sincerity and Target oriented approach & good deeds | | | |

### A. General

i. These Siddha NamaYoga Natives have the nodes Ketu& Rahu as Yogi-Avayogi.

ii. If they also have Sarpa Dosha in their natal chart-its impact will be stronger. However, this Sarpa Dosha impact will be more pronounced after marriage-not when remaining single.

B. Example: 1 – Chart for a Native born **in Siddha Yoga.**

| | Venus<br>Ketu | | |
|---|---|---|---|
| | | | |
| Lagna | | | |
| | | Rahu | |

   i. Lagna: Capricorn, Ketu, Venus in Aswini Nakshatra, Rahu in Swati Nakshatra-The Nodes in their own Stars. Running Dasha (MD) – Mars. Venus MD crossed long back

  ii. Venus & Ketu are posited in the same degree in the Yogi star – This normally portends lot of litigation and other problems including separation.

iii. Because they are in Yogi Star, the spouse got separated from the native-without going to the court. She also allows the Natives family members to see, interact with her children – but does not allow the Native to have access to the children.

 iv. This conjunction, gave physical separation but without resorting to the legal recourse-because placed in Yogi's star.

  v. **Also the Retrograde planets (Nodes) if, posited in the star of Avayogi – reduce their maleficence by half. However, if the Nodes are in Upachaya houses-they dole out their benefic effects multifold.**

 vi. **If there more planets posited in Yogis star – Powerful Yogam. If there are no planets in the star of Avayogi-it's weak, hence less malefic.**

   vii.  This Native had 3 planets in Yogi's star (Ketu, Venus& Mars) and hence powerful Yogi.

  viii.  Note:

- ✓ The Yogi is strong, if there are planets in in its star
- ✓ If a retrograde planet is in Yogis star-that retro planet gains strength
- ✓ The Avayogi is strong, if there are planets in in its star
- ✓ If a retrograde planet is in Avayogi's star-that retro planets becomes weaker

# 22. Sadhya Yoga

| Yogi Star | Yogi | Avayogi Star | Avayogi |
|---|---|---|---|
| Bharani | Venus | Vishaka | Jupiter |

Sadhya Characteristics

Venus (Bharani) is the Yogi and Jupiter (Vishaka) is the Avayogi –

- ➢ They rise through Hard work & attain great heights – Self Made.
- ➢ They are skilled in Arts related matters and profession especially Music
- ➢ They may have relatives from dad side who are sick/deficient in Health/ had unnatural death/without marriage/progenies etc.

In General:

- ➢ This is an Auspicious Yoga which implies fulfillment – Any kind of Meditation/Sadhana could be commenced in this yoga – for good results
- ➢ The children can commence their Study/Education in this yoga – to achieve favorable outcome
- ➢ These Natives get what want – through the process of Sadhana – A dedicated effort. Hence achieve financial success and social status too
- ➢ They are Hardworking, Focused and diplomatic as well. They are efficient, Joyful, humble & smart – Hence always taste success with Sadhana like Mantra/Tantra and the blessings of their worshipped deity

> They are knowledgeable & devoted – yet may not get appreciation from others – Rather beget envy and enmity
> They are confident, patient and take conscious decisions – hence they wait for the results without avoidable worries

## A. General

    i. These Sadhya Namayoga Natives have both the Guru's – Venus & Jupiter as Yogi-Avayogi. If they are conjunct in their chart-it indicates the possibility of a strong Bad karma – already happened or in waiting.

    ii. The planets, transiting over Venus star Purvashada (in Jupiter's sign-SAG) and Jupiter's star Vishaka (in Venus sign-Libra) during the MD-AD of Venus-Jupiter/ Jupiter-Venus, actionise important life events for this Sadhya Namayoga native (Check Example 1)

## B. Example: – Chart for a Native born in **Sadhya Yoga.**

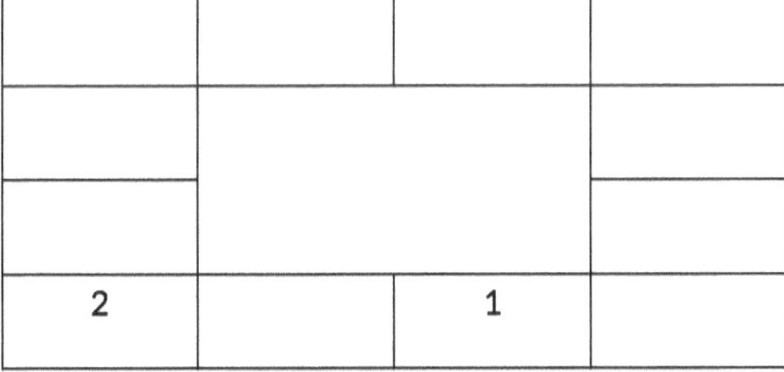

|  |  |  |  |
|---|---|---|---|
|  |  |  |  |
|  |  |  |  |
| 2 |  | 1 |  |

    i. The Conjunction of Venus-Jupiter will, certainly inflict malefic results, esp. in their MD-AD sub periods However, if no Major planets transit over Purvashada/ Vishaka, during these dasha-bukti, No problems. Also no worries, if the Native is not going to encounter their MD-AD periods in future. 1 = Vishaka, 2 = Purvashada.

C.  Example: 1 – Chart for a Native born **in Sadhya Yoga.**

|  |  | Lagna |  |
|---|---|---|---|
|  | **Sadhya Yoga.** |  |  |
|  |  | Jupiter, Venus |  |

i.   Lagna: Taurus, both Jupiter and Venus in Vishaka in Libra & born in Sadhya yoga. Accordingly Venus is the Yogi & Jupiter is the Avayogi. Running Dasha is Jupiter MD.

ii.  Here the $6^{th}$ Lord Venus is in 6H &$8^{th}$ lord Jupiter strongly placed in its own star in 6H. The presence of Avayogi in Yogi's house is a kind of Graha – yuddha. This placement is a strong signifier of a malefic event. The native underwent a surgery of liver transplant & living a sort of life, recovered from the jaws of death.

D.  **Natives with Jupiter as Avayogi:**

i.   If they have Jupiter-Saturn conjunction or a strong Jupiter in their Natal chart – should be advised to be moderate, cautious in eating-food habits.

ii.  Jupiter is the karaka for consumption of food & Saturn is the karaka for digestion. As Jupiter is the Avayogi here, they are susceptible to stomach related chronic ailments – even fatal ones during their MD-AD combine.

iii. Natives with Jupiter as Yogi may not get to suffer these ailments resultant to indigestion, binge-Junk eating etc.

iv.  If the Yogi is posited in the Avayogi star, it does not dole out high benefits, but reduces the strength of Avayogi – to cause harm. Its energy gets dissipated, in just protecting the Native from the Avayogam, however.

v. Jupiter & Saturn are the main karakas for eating – Jupiter for eating a good variety of tasty food & Saturn for old, junk food. Saturn does not want to waste food & hence the provocation to eat stale& old junk food

## 23. Shubha Yoga

| Yogi Star | Yogi | Avayogi Star | Avayogi | Remarks |
|---|---|---|---|---|
| Kritika | Sun | Anuradha | Saturn | |
| **Shubha Characteristics** | | | | |

Sun (Kritika) is the Yogi and Saturn (Anuradha) is the Avayogi –

- ➢ They attain good Name and Fame and Status – Wealth etc.
- ➢ They love and care Female folks & are fairly happy.
- ➢ They may face Problems from Colleagues, bosses as well – disaffection in profession

In General:

- ➢ As the Name suggests, this is a highly auspicious yoga.
- ➢ Any good work executed in this yoga – signifies growth & positivity. Hence the person gets popular and recognized in his chosen field
- ➢ These Natives are Virtuous, Soft, Truthful, Flexible and good hearted – generous
- ➢ They are fortunate, wealthy and free from any financial adversity
- ➢ They are highly respected in the society and may get position and recognition from Govt and allied authority including employment.
- ➢ They respect the Learned, Religious & Saintly people and get respected by all
- ➢ They are beautiful, Smart and skillful & have a pleasant dispensation

A. General

   i. These **Shubha Namayoga** Natives have Sun & Saturn as Yogi-Avayogi. For the – LEO Ascendant Natives born under this yoga, It indicates the possibility of a strong bad karma through any planet placed in the Uttrashada star in Capricorn – viz. already inflicted or in waiting,

   ii. The planets, transiting over Suns star Uttrashada (in Saturn's sign of – CAP) during the MD-AD of Sun-Saturn/Saturn-Sun, Actionise important life events for this Sadhya NamaYoga native(Check Example

   iii. **Illustration Chart** for the above Native born in **Shubha Yoga.**

| | | | |
|---|---|---|---|
| | | | |
| *Uttrashada | Lagna | | |
| | | | |

B. Example: 1 – Chart for a Native born in **Shubha Nama Yoga** – Female born in 1995-Kritika masa

| Moon | | Lagna | |
|---|---|---|---|
| | | | |
| | Shubha Yoga – Natal | | |
| | Sun | | |

i. Lagna: Taurus, Moon in Pisces – Uttrabhadrapada Nakshatra (Saturn's star), Yogi Sun in Avayogi star – Anuradha of Saturn.

ii. Sun is the Yogi & Saturn is the Avayogi for this Shubha yoga born native

iii. This Female always used to find fault with her father.

iv. Thus if a Yogi planet is placed in the star of the Avayogi, all the good actions in line with its positive significations are, neither recognized/appreciated. In many cases, even such positive-well intentioned actions may end up as detriment to the native.

v. All the discussions of the father with his daughter only resulted in pain & tears, mostly Self-inflicted.

C. Example: 2 – Native born in **Shubha Nama Yoga –**

|  |  | Lagna |  |
|---|---|---|---|
|  | Shubha Yoga Natal |  |  |
|  | Sun Saturn |  |  |

i. Lagna: Taurus, Yogi Sun& Avayogi Saturn, conjunct in Avayogi star – Anuradha for this Shubha Nama yoga born native. He was running Sun MD.

ii. This native asks – if he can build a temple in his Purvikam viz. Ancestral/Native place.

iii. **It is to be noted that the Yogi-Avayogi determine only the Activities in their MD-AD combine – but don't impact-change the gunas-nature.**

iv. As he has the Yogi-Avayogi conjunct in his chart & the Yogi is posited in the star of Avayogi, he was advised not to proceed with this initiative. He was also cautioned that, even though his intentions are genuine, it will not be appreciated or recognized in the right perspective & that his image-prestige may take a beating.

v. Despite this, he just goes ahead, constructs a grand temple & completes it.

vi. At the end – he was accused of embezzlement of temple funds& implicated in a scandal. Now, he is restrained from visiting the very temple that came through his own efforts.

vii. He was running the Sun MD at that time – As it is placed in the star of Saturn – signifying Ancestry & Sun-a leader/creator – it allowed him to indulge & complete this Dharmic initiative. But its placement in the Avayogi star &in conjunction with the Avayogi – resulted in loss of reputation

viii. **Suggestion**: We must always observe the Gochara-transit. Had he constructed this temple – when the Sun/Saturn were not transiting over the star Uttrashada – he would have been saved from this ignominy

ix. **# Sun-Saturn conjunction always indicates some Purvika-Ancestral karmic baggage, irrespective of the Nama yoga. This Shubha Nama yoga – implies a bit more of such a Karmic debt.**

## 24. Shukla/Subrahma Yoga

| Yogi Star | Yogi | Avayogi Star | Avayogi |
|-----------|------|--------------|---------|
| Rohini | Moon | Jyeshta | Mercury |
| **Shukla Characteristics** | | | |

Moon (Rohini) is the Yogi and Mercury (Jyeshta) is the Avayogi

➤ May encounter problems from maternal uncle (Krishna – Kamsa) – Displacement from Purvika.

➤ They are short tempered. They may suffer in a particular half of life – young/middle/old age

➤ They may have Self Pride, May face insults/neglect from their off springs and inclined towards joint wealth

In General:

➤ This is also an auspicious yoga & good for Muhurta. Any Work can be commenced in this for favorable outcome. This Yoga signifies Moon.

➤ These Natives have a bright dispensation, creative with an artistic bent of mind

➤ They love poetry and are cultured and courageous! They command love and respect from others in their Circle because of their Artistic pursuits

➤ They are intellectuals – learner of Scriptures & highly qualified. They accumulate good wealth through legal means, Truthful and are good at debates and public speaking

➤ On the flip side – they may also incur the wrath of people who are envious of their stature & prosperity.

### A. General

   i. **Moon** is the Yogi for these Shukla Nama yoga natives & if it's placed in its exalted-Mool Trikona star of Rohini, gets more strength & doles out great benefits. If in its Avayogi star of Jyeshta, afflicts the body & mind apart from blocking about 40% of Yogam-benefit.

ii. If Yogi Moon is conjunct Avayogi Mercury – in any of Mercury's star – it afflicts more.

iii. A native born in Gemini-Virgo Lagna/Rashi and is the youngest in the family – gets afflicted, more than others. Also they get depressed/weakened more, if fail in love matters.

B. Example: 1 – Chart for a Native born in **Shukla Nama Yoga** (She is the Elder-first daughter in law)

|  |  |  |  |
|---|---|---|---|
|  | Shukla Nama yoga |  |  |
|  | Mercury,<br>Moon |  |  |

i. Yogi Moon in Scorpio – Jyeshta Nakshatra and is Conjunct with Avayogi Mercury, in Jyeshta Nakshatra.

ii. The Natives Mother in law is always prone to find fault with her & also dislikes her

C. Example: 2 – Chart for a Native born in **Parigha Nama Yoga** (She is the Younger – Second daughter in law)

|  |  |  |  |
|---|---|---|---|
|  | Parigha Nama yoga |  |  |
|  | Mercury,<br>Moon |  |  |

i. Here too Moon is in Scorpio – Jyeshta Nakshatra and

is conjunct with Mercury there. The Native is naughty & mischievous too. But this Natives Mother in law just ignores her tantrums & is at peace with her.

ii. This is because for this **Parigha** yoga native – No planets in Yogi & Avayogi stars and the Yogi Moon is not afflicted here. Hence, she feels very much at home – in the in-laws house.

iii. Moon, the Karaka for Mother in law – is in the star of Avayogi in the 1st case, which however is not the Avayogi star for the 2nd daughter in law.

iv. While matching the, in laws Horoscopes – (Sambhandi Porutham) with each other-if we encounter Sun-Saturn conjunction it signifies misunderstanding with in laws. Many Marriages break up in India – because of such incompatibility/lack of Synastry with in laws-Parents horoscopes

## 25. Brahma Yoga

| Yogi Star | Yogi | Avayogi Star | Avayogi | Remarks |
|---|---|---|---|---|
| Mrigashira | Mars | Moola | Ketu | |

| Brahma Yoga |
|---|

Mars (Mrigashira) is the Yogi and Ketu (Moola) is the Avayogi

➢ They are Very Agile with Multi-faceted skills & Good in Multi-tasking.

➢ Also Very creative – Can create something from nothing.

➢ They tend to be very helpful to others and liberal in spending.

➢ Possible Depression/Mental health issues to Either the native or his family member

In General:

> This is a very auspicious yoga, which signifies Wisdom and Divinity
> This is the best yoga to resolve any differences, fights and disputes etc. and thereby emerge a winner
> They are very studious, pious, and proficient in Vedic scriptures, Religion and Spirituality and other topics too
> They are virtuous, peaceful, respectable and generous by nature
> They are brave and adventurous too and are ready for any sacrifice to attain higher life purpose – Wisdom and life divine

## A. General

i. Mars-Ketu conjunction indicates, a Dosha-affliction prima facie. This Dosha is more virulent for these Brahma Nama yoga born natives.

ii. The affliction is more for the females than male natives (As Mars is the kalatra karaka for females).

iii. If this conjunction happens in Moola star – it signifies a Dur-Marana (tragic demise) in the family.

iv. Model Chart – for Brahma yoga

| | *Aswini | | |
|---|---|---|---|
| | Brahma Nama yoga | | |
| | | | #Magha |
| *Moola | | | |

*High affliction #Marginal affliction

v. The Native born under Brahma yoga – if born in Aswini or Moola Nakshatra gets troubled more. The affliction is less if born under Magha Nakshatra.

vi. Similarly, the planets placed in Aswini-Moola Nakshatra cause more afflictions to these natives.

B. Example: 1 – Chart for a Native born in **Brahma Nama Yoga**

| | | | Jupiter, Ketu |
|---|---|---|---|
| | Brahma Nama yoga | | |
| | | | |
| Lagna | | | |

*Ketu in Mrigashira

i. This native faced huge business losses & was almost bankrupt.
ii. Then he stepped into Ketu MD. Though Ketu-Jupiter Conjunction indicates huge debts – this native got huge infusion of a loan without interest – because Ketu is posited in the Yogi star of Mrigashira.
iii. Thus, revival & resurrection of his business started & got stabilized in due course.

C. Example: 2 – Chart for a Native born in **Brahma Nama Yoga**

| | | | Lagna |
|---|---|---|---|
| | Brahma Nama yoga | | |
| | | | |
| Jupiter | | | |

i. This Brahma yoga Native born in Gemini Ascendant with Jupiter in 7H of Sagittarius & in Avayogi Moola

Nakshatra. Though he is a well-qualified Bachelor, was unable to get married, despite Jupiter's aspect on lagna.

ii. Then he stepped into Ketu MD. The ensuing month-his 90 year old grandma-committed suicide by hanging, complaining of ill treatment by her family. This spoiled the reputation of the family as a whole.

iii. Thus, Jupiter – the lord of 10H-karmasthan posited in the 7H of marriage (in Star – Moola), in the Avayogi MD of Ketu inflicted this calamity of death & consequent postponement of the Natives marriage.

iv. **The planet Jupiter is the Badakesh for Gemini lagna, gained strength by its placement in the Avayogi star& loses its power to dole out the effect of its benefic aspects on Lagna. It gave him the Material benefits but not on the Marital front.**

## 26. Indra Yoga (aka Mahendra Yoga)

| Yogi Star | Yogi | Avayogi Star | Avayogi | Remarks |
|---|---|---|---|---|
| Ardra | Rahu | Purvashada | Venus | |
| **Indra Yoga** | | | | |
| Rahu (Ardhra) is the Yogi and Venus (Purvashada) is the Avayogi | | | | |

- They have Good Imagination, creative & intuitive.
- Good Interest in Fiction, poetry, Creative Writing etc.
- They are Helpful but impatient too.
- Excessive indulgence & consequent problems therefrom.
- Inability to enjoy even if endowed with goodies

> In General:
>
> - This yoga is good for commencing any work – but only during the day time. Not effective during night
> - The Natives possess a Radiant and the finest personality – leadership, wealthy and fortunate They get to enjoy their family life in full and are unselfish too
> - They are righteous, Caring and skillful and attain excellence in whatever they do – They may turn to be the best/topper in their family Circle
> - On the flipside – their longevity might be short and they may suffer from excessive phlegm and lung issues

## A.  General

i. This **Indra Nama Yoga** is also known as Mahendra Nama Yoga – signifying a child. This signifies some problem in getting a child viz. someone in that family may not beget children.

ii. If these Indra Nama yoga Natives have, Venus-Rahu conjunction-only Rahu delivers all the benefits, not Venus. If Venus too is in retrograde-it diverts the native into bad habits, insolvable problems & may prove fatalistic too.

iii. Also if Venus is in Vargottama – imparts adamancy, expenditures and bad company. The native may turn incorrigible, if it's in a very bad dignity by placement. All due to the Avayogi effect of Venus

B. Example: 1 – Chart for a Native born in **Indra Nama Yoga** (male)

<table>
<tr><td></td><td></td><td>Moon</td><td>Rahu</td></tr>
<tr><td></td><td rowspan="2">Indra Nama yoga</td><td></td></tr>
<tr><td></td><td>Lagna</td></tr>
<tr><td></td><td></td><td></td><td></td></tr>
</table>

i. Leo Lagna, Moon in 10H in Taurus (Kritika star) and Yogi Rahu in 11H of Gemini in Ardra-the Yogi Nakshatra.

ii. In his very youth-got into huge debt, because of wrong administrative decisions. Even forsaken by his close relations.

iii. Then stepped into the Yogi Rahu MD. All of a sudden, all his administrative decisions turned highly successful & yielded massive profits.

iv. Not only he got revived but expanded his business into several verticals, all yielded high gains. All Thanks to the Yogi Rahu – posited in its yogi star of Ardra.

# 27. Vaidhriti Yoga

| Yogi Star | Yogi | Avayogi Star | Avayogi | Remarks |
| --- | --- | --- | --- | --- |
| Punarvasu | Jupiter | Uttrashada | Sun | |
| **Vaidhriti Yoga** | | | | |
| Jupiter (Punarvasu) is the Yogi Sun (Uttrashada) is the Avayogi.<br><br>➢ Hence have good Composure – Good Teacher/Guide to others.<br>➢ Honest and like wearing good ornaments | | | | |

> Problems to Dad & Self in profession
> Possible punishment from Authorities/Govt

In General:

> This is not so an auspicious yoga – not good for traveling. Only such works which are fixed, stable should be carried out – not anything involving travel etc.
> These Natives possess a restless, dynamic and unpredictable yet – a versatile character. Their disorderliness induces difficulties in work & getting socially recognized
> They are good spirited, capable and hardworking and cheerful. They are helpful and charitable – yet they may not get due recognition for their work
> They are prone to physical pleasures and enjoyment – water sports etc. Also enjoy Good dresses & modern outfits etc. and are wealthy too.
> Like Venus – they possess an altogether different/unusual vision of life
> They believe in Religious texts and Spiritual books – yet find it difficult to overcome negative thoughts and secret desires

A. **General**

   i. The chart of the Natives born in this **Vaidhriti yoga** – with Jupiter & Sun conjunction (Yogi-Avayogi Conjunct) indicates the possibility of Kidney ailments/ cancer.

| | | | |
|---|---|---|---|
| | | | |
| | Vaidhriti Nama yoga | | |
| *Jupiter | | | |

*in Uttrashada

ii. If Jupiter is in its own SAG sign in Uttrashada star (Avayogi star)-loses its yogi effect & becomes Neutral. It tempers the Avayogi effect of Uttrashada too. Also, if there is another planet in Libra in Swati Nakshatra, Jupiter turns into a malefic too

iii. Ex: Jupiter in Uttrashada & Moon in Swati for Vaidhriti NamaYoga Native – such a Jupiter is Harmful

| | | | | | | |
|---|---|---|---|---|---|---|
| | Vaidhriti Nama yoga | | | | Gochara-Transit | |
| Jupiter | | Moon | | | | Mars |

iv. If Ketu transits over the Natal Jupiter in Uttrashada – it traps the Native into heavy debt.

v. We have already stated that this Jupiter in Avayogi star – Uttrashada is not beneficial for this Vaidhriti Namayoga

vi. This trouble gets amplified with Jupiter in Uttrashada – gets transited by a planet over Swati in Gochara.

vii. If this Native is in Sun MD, with Sun in Uttrashada (Avayogi) – and Yogi Jupiter transits over Swati in Gochara-it inflicts insurmountable problems to the native. Even the remedies resorted to during this period, don't yield much relief

## Part II: General Attributes of Nama Yogas with Common Yogi & Avayogi

Let us briefly discuss the common Attributes of Certain group of Nama yogas – Holding Identical Lordships of Yogi-Avayogi combination as tabulated under:

| Chapter – Grouping of Nama Yogas on the basis Yogi-Avayogi Planets | | | |
|---|---|---|---|
| Group No | NamaYoga – with Similar Yogi-Avayogi | Common Yogi | Common Avayogi |
| 1 | Athiganda-Vajra-Shukla | Moon | Mercury |
| 2 | Sukarma-Siddhi – Brahma | Mars | Ketu |
| 3 | Dhriti-Indra-Vyatipata | Rahu | Venus |
| 4 | Shoola-Variyan-Vaidhriti | Jupiter | Sun |
| 5 | Ayushman-Dhruva-Siddha | Ketu | Rahu |
| 6 | Vishkumba-Parigha-Ganda | Saturn | Moon |
| 7 | Shiva-Vriddhi – Preeti | Mercury | Mars |
| 8 | Saubhagya-Vyaghata-Sadhya | Venus | Jupiter |
| 9 | Shobana-Harshana – Shubha | Sun | Saturn |

### 1. NamaYoga: Athiganda, Vajra, Shukla

> Moon is the Yogi& Mercury, the Avayogi for the above 3 NamaYoga Natives.

> If Moon & Mercury are in close conjunction – the Yoga – benefits may not fructify.

> The Native suffers on account of unilateral decisions

> The Natives who suffered due to one sided failed love matters – mostly have this Yoga.

> Here Mind is more dominant than intelligence & reason – hence sufferings due to lack of planning

> They encounter problems from Natives with dominant Mercury attributes or Names

- ➤ The MD-AD periods of Moon – Mercury/Mercury-Moon are very challenging & frustrating.
- ➤ The planets posited in the Mercury star in Moon sign or Moons star in Mercury sign – cause a confused, ill planned & indisciplined nature to these yoga Natives.

## 2. NamaYoga: Sukarma, Siddhi, Brahma

- ➤ Mars is the Yogi & Ketu is the Avayogi for the above 3 Namayoga Natives.
- ➤ If Mars & Ketu are in close conjunction in the chart, The Yoga – Benefits don't fructify.
- ➤ The problems are more pronounced – in Family, Spouse & Property matters
- ➤ These Natives encounter troubles from the Mars-Ketu attributes/Named dominant Natives
- ➤ The problems are more pronounced during the sub periods of Mars – Ketu MD – AD or Ketu – Mars MD – AD Periods. These are very challenging times
- ➤ The planets posited in the Ketu star Aswini in Mars sign of Aries, inflict a confused, ill planned & indisciplined nature to these yoga Natives

## 3. Namayoga: Dhriti, Indra, Vyatipata

- ➤ Rahu is the Yogi & Venus, the Avayogi for the above 3 Namayoga Natives.
- ➤ If Rahu & Venus are in close conjunction – the Yoga – benefits may not fructify.
- ➤ They encounter problems from Natives with dominant Venus attributes or Names
- ➤ The MD – AD periods of Venus – Rahu/Rahu--Venus are very challenging & frustrating & even the other yogas obtained normally – are not enjoyed

> ➤ The planets posited in the Swati star in Libra, Venus sign, cause a confused, ill-planned & indisciplined nature to these yoga Natives.

> ➤ If Rahu – Venus is conjunct, Rahu is less harmful but Venus is more virulent – though it's a natural Benefic. In general, this is not a Benefic Conjunction.

> ➤ However, a female native with Rahu – Venus conjunction under this Namayoga – did get a good guidance through her illegal friend – partner.

## 4.  Namayoga: Shoola, Variyan, Vaidhriti

> ➤ Jupiter is the Yogi & Sun is the Avayogi for the above 3 Namayoga Natives.

> ➤ If Jupiter & Sun are in close conjunction in the chart – The Yoga – Benefits don't fructify.

> ➤ The problems are more pronounced – in Health, Possible genetic afflictions like seizure, Cancer etc.

> ➤ Exposure to Sun & Shiva worship are favourable.

> ➤ It's better if they give up, if in any lead position – in Temple related Trusts etc.

> ➤ The Natives in these yoga – if associated in lead, cause few mishaps & disputes

> ➤ These Natives encounter troubles from the Sun related Attributes/Names dominant natives

> ➤ The problems are more pronounced during the sub periods of Sun – Jupiter or Jupiter – Sun MD – AD periods. These are very challenging times

> ➤ The planets posited in the Sun's star of Uttrashada in Jupiter's sign of SAG, cause a confused, ill planned & indisciplined life to these yoga Natives

5. **Namayoga: Ayushman, Dhruva, Siddha**

> Ketu is the Yogi & Rahu is the Avayogi for the above 3 Namayoga Natives.

> These Natives need to worship – Snake pits in the plain region on the ground – Naga worship for better results

> The MD – AD periods of Ketu – Rahu/Rahu--Ketu are very challenging, frustrating & even the other yogas obtained normally – are not enjoyed

> They Encounter problems from Natives with dominant Rahu attributes or Names

> Note: Generally for the Natives with both Nodes as Yogi – Avayogi, the family may be subjected to some sort of a disgrace – esp. during their Dasha sub periods in Combine.

6. **Namayoga: Vishkumbha, Parigha, Ganda**

> Saturn is the Yogi & Moon is the Avayogi for the above 3 Namayoga Natives.

> If Saturn & Moon are in close conjunction in the chart – The Yoga – Benefits don't fructify.

> They should worship Shani's Deities more – for favourable outcome.

> These Natives encounter troubles from the Moon attributes/Names dominant Natives

> The problems are more pronounced during the sub periods of Saturn – Moon or Moon – Saturn MD – AD periods. These are very challenging times

> The planets posited in the Saturn's star of Pushya in Moons sign of Cancer & Moons star of S'ravana in CAP, cause a confused, ill planned and indisciplined life to these yoga Natives.

> The Impact of Punarbhu Dosha is more impactful for these Yoga Natives, than others

## 7. Namayoga: Shiva, Vriddhi, Preeti

> Mercury is the Yogi & Mars is the Avayogi for the above 3 Namayoga Natives.

> If Mercury & Mars are in close Conjunction in the chart – Yoga benefits don't fructify.

> They are better advised to get married early, when young.

> These Natives – if had any premarital love affairs – will still retain & remember those past moments. The Yogi Mercury – even if weakly placed in the chart – still does good

> They Encounter problems from Natives with dominant Mars's attributes or Names

> The MD – AD periods of Mars-Mercury & Mercury-Mars are very challenging & frustrating & even the other yogas obtained normally – are not enjoyed

> Male Natives born in these yogas, if beget a Model younger sister – with a good life, the Natives life happens to be bit challenging & troublesome.

> If the Female Natives get a good lover, the spouse becomes troublesome (Even if she marries the same lover – they turn hostile after sometime).

> They get good & secure friends. They get to enjoy a good love life but a not a very harmonious marital life!

## 8. Namayoga: Saubhagya, Vyaghata, Sadhya

> Venus is the Yogi & Jupiter is the Avayogi for the above 3 Namayoga Natives.

> If Venus & Jupiter are in close conjunction in the chart – The Yoga Benefits don't fructify.

- ➢ The Conjunction of Jupiter & Venus in their charts indicates the curse of a pregnant woman.
- ➢ These Natives encounter troubles from the Jupiter dominant Natives & Guys names like Prakash, Anand and Santosh etc.
- ➢ The problems are more pronounced during the sub periods of Jupiter – Venus & Venus – Jupiter MD – AD periods. These are very challenging times & even the yogas promised otherwise – are not enjoyed or felt.
- ➢ Even though both Jupiter & Venus are high Benefics & Yogic planets – the Natives born in the above Nama Yogas – get either good material benefits or subjective ones viz. Relationship – Life significations – **but not both**
- ➢ These Natives with Yogi-Avayogi Conjunction are bound to suffer from Stree Shraap.

## 9. Namayoga: Shobana, Harshana, Shubha

- ➢ Sun is the Yogi & Saturn is the Avayogi for the above 3 Namayoga Natives.
- ➢ If Sun& Saturn are in close conjunction in the chart – The Yoga – Benefits don't fructify.
- ➢ The Conjunction of Sun & Saturn in their charts indicate possible affliction in the fertility – like Sperm count etc.
- ➢ The Male Natives of these yogas – have problems with their Father, but the Female ones feel the proximity of their Father – missing & long for it, after their marriage!
- ➢ These Natives encounter troubles from the Sun dominant Natives & Names
- ➢ The problems are more pronounced during the sub periods of Sun – Saturn & Saturn – Sun, MD – AD periods. These

are very challenging times & even the yogas promised otherwise – are not enjoyed or felt.

➢ These Yoga born Natives, are prone to Pitri Dosha. Also don't get to enjoy the Ancestral properties/wealth.

➢ Males tend to suffer from Father, Father in law or bosses at work place.

❖ ❖ ❖

## Part III: Yogi – Avayogi: How they play out? – An Astrological Perspective

*****

## 1. Example Chart of a Native in Siddha Nama Yoga.

| | | | Ketu, Jupiter 22°.00 |
|---|---|---|---|
| | Siddha Nama Yoga Yogi-Ketu, Avayogi – Rahu | | Sun 17°30' |
| | | | |
| Lagna/Mars 2°, Rahu | | Saturn 10.°01' | |

*This Native has her Sun in Aslesha in Cancer & the Mudakku (Sthambana) Rashi in Taurus (Kritika), which is in the 6H from Lagna.

i. This Native got Married during the Dasha of Yogi Ketu posited in the 7H.The Native is of dark complexion with good looks.

ii. Her spouse is very fair & handsome. As her yogi Ketu is posited in 7H in Yogis star – She got a very Handsome, Spiritual & Dharmic spouse – from the same faith.

iii. Had Ketu been an Avayogi & in 7H, possibly she might have married a person of an alien faith.

iv.  She has her Kalatra Karaka Mars in Yogis star& in Low Degree (LD) – Hence committed in love to spouse.

v.  She also has Saturn in her Avayogi star. Hence both Yogi& Avayogi are in equal strength.

vi.  The Yogi gains strength when Mars & Ketu transit in Ketu's star in Gochara. The Avayogi gains strength when Saturn & Rahu transit over Rahu's star in Gochara.

vii.  She lost her spouse in Saturn-Rahu MD-AD. The impact was specifically in Rahu AD only not in entire Saturn MD.

viii.  Rahu AD was very virulent for this native

- ➢ She lost her spouse
- ➢ One child too went missing
- ➢ She lost lot of blood & became anaemic
- ➢ Suffered a fire accident & was hospitalized for long
- ➢ This Native has her 6H in the chart as Mudakku Rashi (Sthambana House). Hence she was not enjoying the significance of 6H.
- ➢ Her Bhagyesh-9L is Sun – which is posited in her 6H of Sthambana. Hence, she got tricked into by the very people who she believed to be good

## 2. Summary

- ➢ If there are no planets in Avayogi star – but planet(s) in Yogi star – it's a Yogic chart – Good.
- ➢ If there are no planets in Yogis star but planet in Avayogi's star – It's an Avayoga chart – Not good
- ➢ The Native may encounter bitterness during such an Avayogi AD periods
- ➢ If the Avayogi is posited in the 9th Lord (9L) star – It will prevent the Native from enjoying the fruits of the benefits doled out by the Bhagyesh – 9L.

- It will give less but extract more labour or give but not allow its enjoyment.
- If the Yogi is posited in the Bhagyesh (9L) star, It gives all its fruit & in time without delay
- If the Yogi is in Retrograde – It tries to give its fruits anyhow – very Adamant
- If the Yogi is in Avayogi's star – it gets restricted & its power to deliver curtailed
- The Avayogi if posited in its own star – Can deliver its maleficence with impunity. It does not care for others but its own
- If the Yogi is in close Conjunction with the Avayogi's star by Degree – All its fruits & efforts will get delivered to the others or opponents or may end up self-defeating

❖ ❖ ❖

## Part IV: How to reduce or subdue the Avayogi impact? – Remedies by Worship.

****

1. The Deities and Temples to be worshipped for subduing the impact of Avayogi are listed below for perusal.
2. This is based on the **Avayogi Star** & If any **planet (s)** is placed therein!
3. **If there are no planets in Avayogi – Star in your chart, no worries!**

| S.No | Avayogi Star+ | Deities & Associated Temples |
| --- | --- | --- |
| 1 | Aswini with Planet | Worship of Ganapathy. Also Saraswati Worship Helps (Saraswati temple in Vaniyambadi) |
| 2 | Bharani with Planet | Ashta Buja Durga Parameshwari (Durga with 8 hands) |
| 3 | Kritika with Planet. | Shri Muruga/Subhramanya – Standalone position (Not with consorts) |
| 4 | Rohini with Planet | Shri Krishna – Standalone deity (There is one such temple in Kanchipuram – Pandava Perumal aka Parthasarathi) |
| 5 | Mrigashira with planet | Shri Chandrachoodeshwar Temple (Shiva with Crescent Moon ) in Hosur, Tamilnadu |
| 6 | Ardra with Planet | Shri Nataraja at Chidambaram or Uttrakosa mangai (near Rameswaram) |
| 7 | Punarvasu with Planet | Shri Rama – standalone position |
| 8 | Pushya with Planet | Shri Dakshina Murthy on Sundays (Thursday for Graha remedies – Sunday for Avayogi remedies) |
| 9 | Aslesha with Planet | Sarpa worship at Snake pits in Ground – Plains |
| 10 | Magha with Planet(s) | Shri Ardha Nariswara/Suryanarayana/ SankaraNarayana/Shri Adhi Narayana & so on [Twin lords like Hari – Hara] |
| 11 | Purvaphalguni with Planets | Srirangam – Temple Mahalakshmi |
| 12 | Uttraphalguni with Planet(s) | Sri Alamelu Manga – Mahalakshmi at Tirupati |
| 13 | Hasta with Planet(s) | Sri Bhuvaneshwari Matha |
| 14 | Chitra with Planet(s) | Shri Chakrathalwar-Sudharshan [There are 2 Purana Temples in Kumbakonam – Sarangapani & Ramaswamy temples of Vishnu – with Shri Sudharshan Murthy sannidhi – Can be worshipped there or at any other Vishnu temple) |

| S.No | Avayogi Star+ | Deities & Associated Temples |
|---|---|---|
| 15 | Swati with Planet(s) | Shri. Lakshmi Narasimha (esp. at Parikkal) |
| 16 | Vishaka with Planet(s) | Shri Subhramanya with Consorts Devasena/ Valli |
| 17 | Anuradha with Planet(s) | Shri.Guruvayurappa (Krishna) |
| 18 | Jyeshta with Planet(s) | Shri.Hayagreeva<br>[There is a famous temple in Chettipuyam – 50 km from Chennai – worship in S'ravana] |
| 19 | Moola with Planet(s) | Shri Hanuman (Standalone) |
| 20 | Purvashada with Planet(s) | Shiva worship in a temple near water resources – pond, river, beach etc. |
| 21 | Uttrashada with Planet(s) | Shri. Ganapathy esp. with Shank(Sea shell) |
| 22 | S'ravana with Planet(s) | Shri.Sankaranarayana |
| 23 | Dhanishta with Planet(s) | Shri Ranganatha (Narayana is reclining posture) |
| 24 | Shatabhisha with Planet(s) | All temples earmarked for Longevity/Yama/ Kaleshwara<br>(Thirukadaiyur – Kalasamhara Murthy) – who blessed Bhakta Markhandeya). Shri Yama Pureshwara Shiva near Coimbatore |
| 25 | Purvabhadrapada with Planet(s) | Kanchi Ekambareshwara (Shiva) |
| 26 | Uttrabhadrapada with Planet(s) | Kashi – Rameswaram, Vishwanatha – Ramanathaswamy Shiva |
| 27 | Revati with Planet(s) | Srirangam Ranganatha – Vishnu |

*The remedies indicated are specific & applicable only if any of the above stars is The Avayogi & at least one planet is placed in that star in your Chart

*The Natives residing far off can worship in a similar temple nearby their residence

## Part V: MUDAKKU

## Mudakku Nakshatra & Rashi (Paralyser-Crippler – Sthambana causer)

A. This concept of **Mudakku** is widely used & prevalent among the Astrologers in south esp. in Tamilnadu. **Mudakku** in general means that, which **Cripples/Paralyses** or causes **Sthambana.**

    i. If any planet is placed in the Mudakku Nakshatra-Star, the Native may not get to benefit from the relationship signified by that planet

    ii. If the Avayogi is in Mudakku star – It becomes a complete Avayogi – Multifold

    iii. If the Yogi is Mudakku Star – It still gives the Yogam but in a detached manner

B. **Mudakku Nakshatra Calculator**

The planet **Sun** is the **Natural Atmakaraka** & forms the basis of calculating this Mudakku Star along with **Dhanur Rashi (Sagittarius)** which is the **Natural Bhagyasthan** of KPC

    i. **Method : 1**

       ✓ Mark the Nakshatra (star) of Sun's placement in the chart

       ✓ Count the Placement of Moola Nakshatra from that. (Take that number)

       ✓ Count that number of Nakshatra from thereafter (i.e. After Moola – from Purvashada).

       ✓ This gives the Mudakku Nakshatra

## ii. **Method : 2**

- ✓ Similarly Count the Rashi of Dhanur(SAG) from the Rashi of Sun's placement & count that number of Rashi from Sagittarius
- ✓ That gives the Mudakku Rashi

C. The list of **Mudakku Star, Rashi & Lordship** are summarized in the following table – based on the Nakshatra placement of SUN in the Natal chart

| | | | | Mapping of NL of Sun & Mudakku NL | |
| --- | --- | --- | --- | --- | --- |
| S. No | Nakshatra (Star) of Sun in Natal Chart | Mudakku Nakshatra | Mudakku Rashi & It's Lord | Nakshatra Lord of Natal Sun | Corresponding Mudakku Star Lord |
| I | 2 | 3 | 4 | 5 | 6 |
| 1. | Aswini | Purva Phalguni | Leo – Sun | Sun | Mercury |
| 2. | Bharani | Magha | | Mercury | Sun |
| 3. | Krittika | Aslesha | Cancer – Moon | Moon | Saturn |
| 4. | Rohini | Pushya | | Saturn | Moon |
| 5. | Mrigashira | Punarvasu | Gemini – Mercury | Mars | Jupiter |
| 6. | Ardra | Ardra | | Jupiter | Mars |
| 7. | Punarvasu | Mrigashira | Taurus – Venus | Rahu | Rahu |
| 8. | Pushya | Rohini | | Venus | Ketu |

| S. No | Nakshatra (Star) of Sun in Natal Chart | Mudakku Nakshatra | Mudakku Rashi & It's Lord | Mapping of NL of Sun & Mudakku NL | |
|---|---|---|---|---|---|
| | | | | Nakshatra Lord of Natal Sun | Corresponding Mudakku Star Lord |
| 1 | 2 | 3 | 4 | 5 | 6 |
| 9. | Aslesha | Kritika | Aries – Mars | Ketu | Venus |
| 10. | Magha | Bharani | | Note1: We can infer from the above that if the placement of Sun is in Suns star – Star of Mercury is Mudakku, if in Saturn star – Moons star is Mudakku & so on. If Sun is in Rahu star – Rahu itself turns Mudakku. | |
| 11. | Purva Phalguni | Aswini | | | |
| 12. | Uttra Phalguni | Revati | Pisces – Jupiter | | |
| 13. | Hasta | Uttra Bhadrapada | | | |
| 14. | Chitra | Purva Bhadrapada | Aquarius – Saturn | | |
| 15. | Swati | Shatabhisha | | | |
| 16. | Vishaka | Dhanishta | Capricorn – Saturn | **Note 2: Avayogi & Mudakku** | |
| 17. | Anuradha | S'ravana | | ➤ If Sun is the Avayogi – Use Mercury to Cripple the Avayogam | |
| 18. | Jyeshta | Uttrashada | Sagittarius – Jupiter | ➤ If Moon is the Avayogi – Use Saturn to Cripple the Avayogam | |
| 19. | Moola | Purvashada | | ➤ If Venus is the Avayogi – Use Ketu to Cripple the Avayogam (Like Worship of Ganesh) Thus for Avayogi Effect Neutralisation – Worship the Overlord of the Relevant Mudakku Star Planet, | |
| 20. | Purvashada | Moola | | | |
| 21. | Uttrashada | Jyeshta | Scorpio – Mars | | |
| 22. | S'ravana | Anuradha | | | |
| 23. | Dhanishta | Vishaka | Libra – Venus | | |
| 24. | Shatabhisha | Swati | | | |
| 25. | Purva Bhadrapada | Chitra | Virgo – Mercury | | |
| 26. | Uttra Bhadrapada | Hasta | | | |
| 27. | Revati | Uttra Phalguni | Leo – Sun | | |
| Note: *Thus We can always use the **Mudakku** Concept by worshipping its Deities to neutralize/counter the impact of the **Avayogi** planet in our chart by equating/ Mapping the Columns 5&6 above* | | | | | |

D. General Snippets

1. **Mudakku** signifies a condition which may not be useful or enjoyed by the Native – Like he does not get to benefits from the relationship signified by the planet placed in Mudakku Nakshatra (star).

2. Ex: If Moon in Mudakku star – He will not get the Love/care of mother.

3. If the Avayogi is in Mudakku Star – the impact gets multiplied & highly Virulent. If the Yogi in Mudakku- gives some benefits but without attachment.

4. **The Remedies for Mudakku Star – are veritable tools to break the impact of the Avayogi**

5. If there are no planets in Mudakku star – Not much adverse impact

6. If the Kalatra Karaka (Mars for female/Venus for Male) are Avayogi's & and in Mudakku star – needs to be very careful in the MD-AD of Avayogi.

7. However, we must keep in mind that the Yogi-Avayogi impacts the life events only in their MD-AD-PAD & Gochara – Not throughout.

8. **It is incumbent on any Astrologer to identify this Mudakku Rashi & Advise remedies so that the Blockages to its signified Bhava are removed**

E. **Mudakku Rashi(Sign) and Bhava related Impact**

**Thumb Rule:** It is always advisable that the Natives remains unattached/Desire less to the Karakatwa of the signified Bhava of Mudakku Rashi-Nakshatra in their Natal chart. They are tabulated in brief as under

| S. No | Mudakku Rashi – Where Mudakku Nakshatra is placed | Dos & Don'ts |
|---|---|---|
| 1. | Lagna – 1H | Refrain from Self Boasting &Excess Make-Up & Show offs. Prone to recurrent troubles – self made |
| 2. | 2H | Refrain from Glorifying the Family & Income in public. Possible issues related to 2H signified matters |
| 3. | 3H | Problems in the Matter of siblings, Initiatives, Property sale-Business sales etc. Also Medical expenses to Siblings. Problems in 3rd H signified matters |
| 4. | 4H | No excess attachment to Mother & Comforts. Medical expenses to mother & problems in 4H signified matters |
| 5. | 5H | No reciprocation of Love from Children & possible sickness to children & grandparents. Even Mantra Siddhi – turns negative – affects health. No Benefit due to Mantra recitation and also don't aspire for Ancestral wealth. |
| 6. | 6H | Problems due to Loans & Maternal uncle, Rivals etc. Even small diseases turn expensive & Maternal uncle unhealthy. General issues from 6H signified Karakatwa. |
| 7. | 7H | Problems through Spouse & business partners. Any effort towards earning from abroad may come a cropper. Medical expenses to Spouse & closed ones. In General – Impacts 7H signified matters |
| 8. | 8H | No success in Occult Matters-No sudden fortune or gains through Luck. No gain from 8H signified matters |
| 9. | 9H | No excess attachment to father and also no independent ventures. Possible Health expenses on father & 9H signified karakatwams. |

| 10. | 10H | High Karmic impact – refrain from taking unilateral decisions in professional matters – Go for collective decisions. Issues from In-laws family & possible ill health to them. Impacts 10H signified karakatwas |
|-----|-----|---|
| 11. | 11H | No obsession with gains-Profits & with elder siblings – Impacts their health & expenses thereof. Affects 11H signified Matters |
| 12. | 12H | Need to be Cautious of Rebound of Past karmas & take advance protection. Possible problems from 12H signified Matters like isolation, Jail, Hospital, Bed comforts etc. |

**It is advisable that this Mudakku Rashi & its Bhava is identified in the Chart & immediate remedial worships resorted to get relief/release from the blockages signified by the Mudakku Bhava&its Lord.

**Mudakku is one Primary reason for Non Fructification of Yogas promised in the Chart.

# CHAPTER 4

# THITHI & THITHI SHUNYA



"AUM GAM GANAPATHAYE NAMAHA"

"AUM GURAVE NAMAHA"

## PANCHANGA & THITHI:

The Use & Functionality of the Panchanga is succinctly described in the following Classical Panchanga Phala Sloka

| The Classical Panchanga Phala Sloka Signifying the use-functionality of Panchanga Elements | |
| --- | --- |
| तिथेश्च श्रियमाप्नोति वारादायुष्य वर्द्धनम्। <br><br> नक्षत्रद्वरते पापं योगाद्रोग निवारणम्। <br><br> करणं कार्य सिद्धिँ च <br> पञ्चाङ्गफलमुत्तमम्।। | Thitheshcha shriyamapnothi vaaradayushya vardhanam <br><br> Nakshatra dwarathe paapam yogadroga Nivaranam <br><br> Karanam karya siddhim cha Panchanga phala muththamam |
| Meaning: <br><br> Knowledge of Thithi bestows Wealth, Knowledge of Vaara increases Longevity, Knowledge of Nakshatra erases Sins, Knowledge of Yoga cures Diseases and Knowledge of Karana ensures Success in work | |

Thus, we can infer that The Panchanga in general is a veritable tool – in – aid to achieve some Dependable Derivations from a Natal chart (Horoscope). Thithi is the Primary Element of the Panchanga and A Karana is half of Thithi – which signifies the modifier impact of the Thithi.

*In Short, a Thithi signifies the Wealth of All kinds (16 types) promised in the chart & the means too. The Karana indicates how it is achieved – like the mode-style and means of one's activity (Karma) – profession and possible success rate.*

## A. THITHI in Brief

1. **Thithi** is among the foremost element of **Panchanga** along with **Nakshatra**. The Thithi is based on the distance between the Sun & Moon. Most of the festivities &

carnivals are celebrated based on Thithi only, apart the Pitri Karya's too. In Medical Astrology – Thithi is used for linking Birth& Death too.

2. **This essentially, reflects the inheritance of Punya-Bhagya from the forefathers, its plus & minuses. Thithi needs to be seen to quantify the Blessings/Ashirvad & Thithi – Shunya (Daghda) – mostly for progeny related issues**

3. Thithi is classified under 2 Groups – Shukla Paksha (Waxing) and Krishna Paksha (Waning) Thithi(s). Thithi plays an important role in Jyotish esp. in Prashna. The Thithi in which – someone seeks horoscope reading is paramount.

   ✓ If a Native seeks horoscope readings in Ashtami – It indicates Vishnu Shraap viz. – He is short of blessings of Narayana.

   ✓ Ashtami is when both Mercury lorded Rashis are on fire viz. Gemini & Virgo.

   ✓ That's why Most Knowledgeable Astrologers refrain from Offering Consultations on Ashtami

4. **Thithi in Worship for Remedies**

   ✓ There are some Confusion/Controversy in choosing appropriate times of Worships/Remedies-Say, Kartikeya Worship as Prayaschitta/Parihara

   ✓ The Native asks – If he has to do this on Shashti Thithi, Mangal Vaara or in Kritika Nakshatra – All related to Lord Muruga/Kartikeya. First Check the Purpose of worship – seeking Prayaschitta.

   ✓ The logic is as follows.

      ✓ If this is to mitigate the Shraap/Dosha of the past – Choose THITHI. Like seeking the Blessing of Pitris/ Parents – Choose Thithi

- ✓ If it is to mitigate the Current – immediate problems – Choose Nakshatra
- ✓ If it is for future events like Daughter's wedding, Purchase of Property etc. – Choose Vaara – Day.
- ✓ This way, we can demarcate & take up Prayaschitta – Parihara!
- ✓ Thus to come out of the Effect of the Troubles of the Past – Choose THITHI, Present – Nakshatra, Future – Vaara – Day

5. All Routine & General Worships – Shukla – Paksha/Waxing phase **Worship – Rituals are good. For Prayaschitta/ Parihara – Krishna Paksha Worships**

6. **Each Thit**hi indicates/Supports specific pointers

- ✓ Ex: One Native under the Spell of close SAT – MOON conjunction in Capricorn (Punarbhu Dosha). He was facing lot of hurdles & delays in getting married & in all his initiatives.
- ✓ He was suggested: Regular Worship of Ganesh – during Sankata – Hara – Chathurthi.
- ✓ Also Worship During Monday – Shani Hora/Nakshatra/ Saturday – Moon Hora/Nakshatra combos!
- ✓ Had all obstacles removed & leading a blessed marital life.

7. Ekadashi Vrat :

- ✓ This is the best remedy for Females having uterine issues & Progeny. This Vrat-Fasting along with Worship of Female deities.
- ✓ Of course these Vrats are meant for Toxic clearance – not for bodily suffering. Hence Abstinence from eating

only to the extent of tolerance capacity – not over stretching.

✓ This combined with Upasana – gives wonderful outcomes

8. Dashami Thithi: This is most favourable for commencement of any new Business/Work including Study. That's why Vijaya Dashami is considered the most auspicious. However, we must ensure that the running AD is not of the planet in THITHI Shunya. If it is – better to wait for the Dashami in Next AD

9. Panchami Thithi is good for – Mantra Siddhi & Ashtami for Sarpa Dosha remedies

10. Thithi in Matchmaking

   ✓ It is not advisable to Match 2 charts born on the same Thithi – as they will have the same Thithi Shunya

   ✓ Also avoid matching two charts with Taurus/Libra ( 2H&7H of KPC) in Daghda-Thithi Shunya

   ✓ Both Charts having LEO (5H of KPC) in Thithi Shunya – to be avoided viz. Shashti Thithi Born should not be matched, as both 1H & 5H of KPC are in Thithi Shunya to avoid Progeny issues.

**B. Thithi Shunya in Brief:**

1. All the 14 Thithi's – barring Purnima, Amavasya – cast, a Daghda-Burnt out effect on certain Rashis-signs of the

zodiac. These, burnt out Rashis are believed to be in THITHI SHUNYA on those respective Thithi(s), as tabulated at the end of this chapter.

- ✓ The Thithi Shunya Rashis are indicated as Daghda Rashis (Under Fire) in our Horoscope.
- ✓ Thithishunya Rashi – Primarily indicates Forefathers/Pitris Curse & Pain.
- ✓ It may be noted that those born in Purnima/Amavasya do not suffer Thithishunya. This indicates that the good karma of the Native has an overriding impact
- ✓ The Pain of our Pitris gets transmitted through Thithishunya Rashis. The Planets placed therein, fail to give their effects.
- ✓ The Thithi Shunya Rashi(s), if tenanted by more planets, indicate lack of Ancestral blessings.
- ✓ Hence Pitris worship is paramount to overcome.
- ✓ If Thithi Shunya Rashi – has no planets – Indicates good blessings & Hence the Native should continue to perform Dharmic activities to retain/sustain that.
- ✓ Thithishunya is Stronger than the Massa Shunya (The month of birth – not auspicious for Shubha Karya like Marriage)
- ✓ Thithi Shunya indicate one's desire
- ✓ Thithi Shunya effects are more Subjective-like Relationship – Progeny oriented – Don't affect Material Significations like wealth/income etc.
- ✓ If there are no planets in Thithishunya – Good (best option) – No denial of fruits – but it's delivery after some pain.

2. **Thithi Shunya (TS) Thumb rule**

   ✓ Check if the planet in TS is a Benefic/Malefic (KP Moon/ Retro JU & ME too are Asubha)
   ✓ **Benefics in TS fail to deliver anything good**
   ✓ **Malefics in TS fail to cause any Harm**

3. **THITHI SHUNYA (TS): Understanding of – in Practical Life**

   i. Thithi Shunya Rashi(s) indicate one's desire

      ✓ Ex : Pratipda Thithi born : Libra/Capricorn in TS – The 7H/10H of KPC indicates More Desire towards Relationship+ Profession
      ✓ Ashtami: Gemini & Virgo in TS – Indulgence in constant communication talkative. It also indicates Vishnu Shraap.
      ✓ If Aries sign is in Thithishunya – The Native tend to aspire for Anonymous wealth

   ii. Karana Lord (Panchanga) – KL is the Karya Karta for execution & ensures Karya-siddhi.

      ✓ If the KL is in TS – He helps in the fructification of desires – Neutralises the TS effects

   iii. Malefics/Badakesh, in Thithishunya are welcome – Maleficence is reduced (it's like the curse of a fake Guru – no strong impact)

      ✓ Malefic in TS if in Retrograde – Still better
      ✓ Malefic in TS – Pardoned of Sins
      ✓ Benefics in TS will cease to do well!!

4. **Major Impact of Thithishunya**

   i. Obstructions in Progeny – Putra Karaka (JU), 5H and 5L if in TS.

ii. Pain & Insults in the matters/Profession relating to TS Rash**is.**

   ✓ Venus in TS – Stree Shraap – curse of a female.

iii. **Thithishunya effects are more Virulent for the Native born in Chaturdashi**. All the 4 corners of the KPC chart – Dual signs 3/6/9/12 are impacted

   ✓ No gainsaying, these are the signs indicating KAPD. The dual signs are indicative of the Jeevas – with human qualities like Serpent etc.
   ✓ Harming Such Animals/Serpents by torture – killing – The concerned Natives get to take birth with these TS in Dual signs.
   ✓ After all Chaturdashi is never considered for any Auspicious Muhurta

iv. Those born in Panchami, Ashtami& Chaturdashi may have some Vishnu Shraap – like their ancestors violated some promise made to the Lord

v. Similarly,those born in Cancer Lagna/Moon & on Saptami- indicates some Stree Shraap – like they had caused harm to a female/pregnant female

vi. Normally 8th lord-8L is a Dire Malefic – He is good in TS.

vii. Lagna Lord if in TS – Causes Stress& Fatigue. Also, LL is in TS or the TS sign lord in Lagna – Low self esteem

viii. TS in 2H – Not much attention to close family esp. – bad relationship with at least one member. Same is True if TS in 11H too

ix. TS in 9H – Good for foreign. Also Badakesh in TS – Nullifies the effect (like if JU is the Badakesh & in TS – does not impede progeny)

x. If LEO signs in TS – Gets Stomach ailments. Perhaps the Father ignored his parents & gets his karma passed on. Similarly the failure of our duties to our Pitris, get transmitted to the concerned Bhava.

xi. If Aries in TS, aspires for Anonymous wealth

xii. Venus in TS – Stree Shraap – curse of a female. Any Native, who cries without reason, may have this. If Venus is with Mandhi – it's a more powerful curse

xiii. If your child has TS in 2H – It nurtures a Feeling of Inadequacy & pain

xiv. Planetary aspects don't play in TS effects

xv. Even Auspicious events signified by the planets – get accomplished with Anxiety & pain, if in TS

xvi. No planets in TS is the best option (No Pitris curse)

xvii. **The effect of planets in TS is more pronounced only in their MD/AD/PAD**

## 5. The Significance of 5H/7H in TS

i. 5H is a Purva Punya sthan. If it's in TS & also its karaka Jupiter in TS – The negatives are well pronounced.

ii. It may give Material gains but damage relationship like Denial/Delays in progeny

iii. Even if a child is born – They Live away from it or problems in getting it Married & resultant pains etc.

iv. In few cases Children with Autism/Drug Addiction etc.

v. TS in 5&8th Houses is sure to give Painful Experience through Progeny. Need to be extra careful during Pregnancy

vi. If 5&8 H are TS for both – The Man should support his spouse 100%.

vii. In One case – The couple – both have TS in 2/5/8/11 – Chaturdashi born. Got a Progeny after some pain – 8 years with the Mother suffering blood losses after delivery. Finally all well, due to God's Grace & Benign Karna Lord Jupiter

viii. Remedy: Sincere prayers & Worship to Pitris & Kula Davata on TS free days – Amavasya & Purnima is the Primary Karmic Cleansing Remedy for TS

ix. 7H is TS with 9L therein who is in Parivartana with 7L – it will give Marriage & children.

- ✓ But the spouse may not be interested in getting a child – delays
- ✓ If not the Native after its birth, may stay away from his child (like working Abroad/Army etc. )
- ✓ Even Lord RAMA – Had this & suffered the above

## 6. TS in a Nutshell (Summary)

I. The Effects are most pronounced in 5H/5L & Putrakaraka Jupiter (Progeny issues) & in 7H to some extent.

- ✓ Impacts matters involving Mind & Relationship
- ✓ Even if granted (of Children/Wife), Lack of emotional connectivity or feeling towards them

II. All the Malefic impacting concepts find their Succour in TS viz.

- ✓ All Natural Malefics including Badakesh, 6-8-12 Lords
- ✓ Retrograde, Debilitated & Combusted planets
- ✓ Avayogi planet & the Nodes Rahu – Ketu
- ✓ Mandhi in 5H – in TS can relieve Stress

**They all lose their Maleficence in TS. <u>Malefic in TS – Pardoned of Sins</u>**

III. If TSL in Indu Lagna : Adverse after effects – separation after Marriage – Disappointment/Feeling cheated etc.

IV.   Thithi Shunya Rashi – If tenanted by more planets – indicates lack of Ancestral blessings. Hence Pitri worship is paramount to overcome.

V.   If Thithi Shunya Rashi – has no planets – Indicates good blessings & Hence the Native should continue to perform Dharmic activities to retain/sustain that. Venus in TS – Stree Shraap – curse of a female.

VI.   **Karana** Helps in Annihilation of Thithi Shunya Blockages. If the KL is in TS – He helps in the fructification of desires – Neutralises the TS effects

VII.   **Tithi Shunya Exceptions**

- ✓ Any Malefic in TS causes No harm & hence is beneficial in general.
- ✓ Yogas caused by Benefics or a Yoga formed by a Quadrant and Trinal lord confers auspicious& satvik blessing's in life (PMPY & DKAY Yogas)
- ✓ Vipareetha Yogas caused by 6 8 12 and Bhadaka lords gives makes one a celebrity and gives name, fame, power, prosperity etc.
- ✓ The Yogas caused by Tithi Shunya Rashi (TS) and planets increases the Vipareetha yoga into a Vipareetha Raja Yoga. This is clearly visible in most of the celebrities
- ✓ **Finally, TS as such does not play any significant role, except in the Matters of Progenies/Relationships Matching – Don't impede Material significations.**

## 7.  Remedies

I.   **Respecting the Parents throughout your life (irrespective of their nature) is the primary duty**

II.   Parents & Guru should bless with their heart out – they should feel pleased 100%

III. Pitri Karma/Worship of the departed Pitris on Amavasya & Purnima and their anniversary Thithi.
IV. Worship & Snan in Holy places like Rameswaram/Kashi/ Prayag/Badrinath/Gaya etc.
V. Prayers to Lord Ganesh – The most dutiful son
VI. A native Complained that All the females in his family face Premature deaths. This gets reflected in all the Female planets placed in Thithi Shunya

- ✓ Ex: AQU Lagna – 5H Gemini in TS – With VE + MOON + ME
- ✓ This indicates Stree Shraap & hence Impedes Progeny
- ✓ He was asked to seek Lakshmi Narayan blessings along with Worship of Female deities & Kanyas. Also respect & help the karakas signified by TS planets – Here Mother, Sisters, and Spouse etc.
- ✓ He was blessed with Twins after 1 year

VII. Frequent Bath in Sea in holy places & in Salt water is also a good remedy
VIII. Performance of **Pavamana – Sukta** homa too helps its mitigation

## 8. Thithi &Thithi Shunya Rashi(Daghda) & General Impact

| Table 1: Thithi &Thithi Shunya Rashi(Daghda) & General Impact | | | |
|---|---|---|---|
| S. No | Thithi | Thishunya Rashi | ➢ General Characteristics of THITHI in Brief |
| 1. | Pratipada | Libra, Capricorn | ➢ Impacts 2H/7H/10H Significations as Venus & Sat are TSL. Hence – Possible struggle in Education, Career and Child etc.<br>➢ If Family life is good – Profession gets affected and vice versa – but not both. They should not work jointly as partners in business.<br>➢ If born in SP – Family needs to be cared & if born in KP – More Focus on career is a must<br>➢ The Natives born in Pratipada under Venus/Saturn Nakshatra could encounter health/relationship issues when Moon transits over them in Gochara.<br>➢ Need to be cautious when Malefics transit over Cap & Libra in Gochara – no important work<br>➢ In general – They do think deeply before acting. |
| 2. | Dwitiya | Sagittarius Pisces | ➢ Impacts 9H/12H Significations as Jupiter is the TSL (also 5H)<br>➢ Dad could be inimical/inflict losses if loving<br>➢ They are fairly Truthful and don't lie. May get cheated – victim of breach of faith.<br>➢ As Guru is the TSL – problems in progeny & Kula Vriddhi or may not get to live with them<br>➢ May not get to enjoy the assets of Dad, But highly attached to Mother<br>➢ Either the children may not get cared for by the parent or vice versa<br>➢ In general live with good comforts |

| Table 1: Thithi &Thithi Shunya Rashi(Daghda) & General Impact | | | |
|---|---|---|---|
| 3. | Tritiya | Leo Capricorn | ➢ Impacts 5H/10H Significations as Sun &Saturn are the TSL(9H too)<br>➢ Worries about children & possible losses from first business<br>➢ Possible enemity, insults from Dad – like Dad dominant, controlling or involved in a Cold war – indirect enemity with him. Possibly a sort of Badakesh<br>➢ Possible roadblocks in family progress – Dad, Ancestry, Progeny issues<br>➢ This Thithi Born Father and daughter should not travel in life together-live away from each other if possible<br>➢ They generally accomplish their desires<br>➢ Good speakers and Communicators |
| 4. | Chathurthi | Taurus, Aquarius | ➢ Impacts 2H/11H Significations as Venus, Saturn are the TSL's.<br>➢ Impacts 7H too.<br>➢ They are highly committed & care for everyone in the family – but get nothing in reciprocation. Only Insults, neglect and no respect<br>➢ Aquarius is TS only for Chathurthi which is the natural Bhadaka house of KPC. Hence highly karmic and gains are very scarce.<br>➢ They don't stay put in one place – Agile and are inclined to learn Mantras too<br>➢ Remedy – Vinayaka Worship on KP-Chathurthi for relief from Insult, Neglect and for good Marital harmony |
| 5. | Panchami | Gemini, Virgo | ➢ Impacts 3H/6H Significations as Mercury is the TSL<br>➢ Mercury is the unique TSL which lords 3H&6H of KPC (Veerya-Dhairya).Hence they may be endowed with very high Physical Strength, Courage, Ability & Health or lack of them (weak) – both in extremes.<br>➢ They have Attachment to the opposite sex (Females). They are prone to fall in love but without much success |

| Table 1: Thithi &Thithi Shunya Rashi(Daghda) & General Impact | | | |
|---|---|---|---|
| | | | ➤ Though endowed with all assets – they may not get to use/enjoy them<br>➤ They are Very intelligent, Skillful in Arts or also the opposite of it (Also dull witted etc. if in bad dignity)<br>➤ They should guard against Ego & Pride – which may lead to their fall from grace<br>➤ They can sacrifice for children & may have debts<br>➤ This Thithi is good for Spirituality and Worship<br>➤ May signify Vishnu Shraap too. |
| 6. | Shashti | Aries, Leo | ➤ Impacts 1H/5H Significations and Both Mars and Sun are the TSL's.<br>➤ Aries Sign is TS only for Shashti Thithi – Lagna of KPC in TS implies that this Thithi is highly karmic, which impacts health and Progeny<br>➤ This Native should not marry another Shashti born Native. Never, ever match this<br>➤ It is bound to lead to problems in progeny like abortion, difficulty in conception &unhealthiness. Even if born & grown – May have to face insults and disrespect – from those children<br>➤ May have land related problems<br>➤ Possible child issues for female & for Males from brothers<br>➤ They may do better if live away from family or home. They are liked by the rich and powerful<br>➤ They are prone to Stomach related ailments including uterus and reproductive organ related, especially if Mars is in Leo.<br>➤ They like snacks & spicy food<br>➤ Interest in politics/govt but may not be successful – They like to travel/tour often |

| Table 1: Thithi &Thithi Shunya Rashi(Daghda) & General Impact | | | |
|---|---|---|---|
| 7. | Saptami | Cancer, Sagittarius | <ul><li>Impacts 4H/9H Significations and both Moon and Jupiter are the TSL's.</li><li>Saptami – **it's a Highly Karmic Thithi** impacting both the Mother and Father. Differences with mom & possible issues in Matrimony</li><li>They may cause separation between their Parents upon their birth or they get to live separately or not so in harmony – Like a Glorified Orphan</li><li>As Moon and Jupiter are TSL – their Conjunction may not do good for them</li><li>**Cancer Sign is TS only for this Thithi** – Hence If born in Cancer lagna with Moon in S'ravana – double whammy.</li><li>They are very sympathetic in general and They do better if relocate outside their nativity – Abroad</li><li>The Remedy: Worship at Suryanarayar Koil – Where the Sun Lord is aspected by both Jupiter from front and Moon from behind.</li></ul> |
| 8. | Ashtami | Gemini Virgo | <ul><li>Impacts 3H/6H Significations and Mercury is the only TSL</li><li>Ashtami is considered inauspicious in South as it's an in between Thithi – Moon and Sun are around 90 degree and considered unstable</li><li>In North, it is considered as auspicious for many new beginnings esp. involving competition etc.</li><li>Mercury is the only TSL (3H-6H of KPC) – Who gives Maraka effect through genetic disorders – However it does not kill.</li><li>They are self-made and come up with struggle around 40 years of age.</li><li>They are intelligent, love children and save well/spend for their welfare too.</li></ul> |

| Table 1: Thithi &Thithi Shunya Rashi(Daghda) & General Impact | | | |
|---|---|---|---|
| | | | ➢ In North, it is counted as an Auspicious Thithi to commence any new creative work – as this has the blessings of Brahma & Lakshmi. Any work involving new creation/creativity could be commenced<br>➢ Karmic impact through Mom's side – Education and nerve issues, Migraine, Mental tension and soon<br>➢ These issues keep cropping up at regular interval – like once a decade<br>➢ If Mercury is in good dignity like a Yogi/ Karana Lord they turn out to be highly creative, artistic & prosper too |
| 9. | Navami | Leo Scorpio | ➢ Impacts 5H/8H Significations and Sun & Mars are the TSL's.Impacts the 9H too<br>➢ The Native loves Name & Fame and may have recurrent issues with father<br>➢ They may not be able to do the Karma Karya of dad (may not be the eldest) or Prevented to perform any rites due to dad.<br>➢ This may continue for generations. Deprived of the benefits of Ancestry.<br>➢ Thus they should not use the dad's wealth or get to enjoy his proximity – without remedial measures<br>➢ Refer – (Story of Rama/Dasratha born in Navami – Dashami) |
| 10. | Dashami | Leo Scorpio | ➢ This Thithi too has significations identical to Navami above (Impacts 5H&8H with Sun & Mars in TS)<br>➢ Native May not get to enjoy the Proximity of his eldest progeny<br>➢ They emerge Victorious in any Competition and this Thithi signifies Victory of Dharma over Evil<br>➢ They relish sweets & could be bald too – Hair issues<br>➢ Losses in business – high admin expenses as Sun & Mars involved<br>➢ They are highly virtuous and disciplined<br>➢ They Keep up their promises |

| Table 1: Thithi &Thithi Shunya Rashi(Daghda) & General Impact | | | |
|---|---|---|---|
| | | | ➤ Impacts 9H/12H Significations as Jupiter is the TSL – Possibly 5H too<br>➤ They are good people, loving and care and work for others – but may get deceived or used by others easily<br>➤ Hard workers, Guide others but they don't rise much or get help from others<br>➤ Jupiter is the TSL – hence worries about children. |
| 11. | Ekadashi | Sagittarius Pisces | ➤ This is virulent for Mercury – Venus sign Ascendants if Jupiter is in good houses. They get Good benefit of JU, if it is in Dustana houses only (Guru in Moon star – indicates the secret of parents indirectly)<br>➤ They are however inclined to Earn and Accumulate material comforts too – though may get to enjoy them only within limits<br>➤ This Thithi is the Most auspicious to undertake fasting and upavasa – for detox and anger management.<br>➤ Prayer during Vaikunta Ekadashi – Helps to prevent this susceptibility to deception – getting passed on to progenies and future generations |
| 12. | Dwadashi | Libra Capricorn | ➤ Impacts 7H/10H Significations as Venus, Saturn are the TSL's and also 2H.<br>➤ Hence should not be in profession/ business in the Native place.<br>➤ Strict – No – to partnership with Spouse or Family members in business, loan or property<br>➤ Working from home is an issue – They May either flourish in Profession or Home-life and not both<br>➤ May get deceived by friends/partners & may even give up his stakes for them<br>➤ In General – they enjoy success in later part<br>➤ They do love venturing into new territories of business |

| Table 1: Thithi &Thithi Shunya Rashi(Daghda) & General Impact | | | |
|---|---|---|---|
| 13. | Trayodashi | Taurus, Leo | ➤ Impacts 2H/5H Significations as Venus, Sun are the TSL's-Possibly 7H too.<br>➤ If Sun and Venus afflicted in the Chart – Family life, Unity, Comforts and life progress – All shall be impacted<br>➤ They despite having relatives – don't get right food clothing etc. – long for good quality of life in childhood/for children – But they do rise in life at a later stage<br>➤ They are Smart – survive through speech<br>➤ They can't stay put in one place<br>➤ Attached to Purvika/temple and long for Dad's love – but may not get to live with close relatives |
| 14. | Chaturdashi | Gemini, Virgo, Sagittarius, Pisces | ➤ All the 4 dual signs fall under TS & all the 4 corners impacted (3H-6H-9H-12H). Both Jupiter and Mercury are TSL's<br>➤ They love foreign languages – Like Arts – have interest in earning n wealth creation & Sacrifice for children<br>➤ Highly Inauspicious and Not a smooth family life<br>➤ Highly Tactful, Cunning and Calculative – can defeat their enemy by sheer tact.<br>➤ They are technically sound and good advisers – but it may not work out favourably for their own benefits<br>➤ This is not Auspicious for doing good work esp. if it's in KP – However good for resolving long pending litigation, disputes<br>➤ Even if endowed with goodies – they don't get to feel or enjoy that<br>➤ They do harbour some vengeance and don't pardon/forget the mistakes that easily-unless Jupiter and Mercury are in good dignity |
| 15. | Amavasya | None | ➤ This is Good for all Pitri Karya – Rituals to Ancestors.<br>➤ Shrardh and Tarpan to ancestors on this day – esp. on water fronts like – Confluence of Rivers and ocean etc. |

| Table 1: Thithi &Thithi Shunya Rashi(Daghda) & General Impact | | | |
|---|---|---|---|
| | | | ➢ The Amavasya falling on Makar-Karkataka Sankranti months and Mahalaya-Pitri Paksha are the most beneficial to seek blessings from Pitris and to offset any Pitri shraap in the chart<br>➢ Though no Thithi Shunya – It's a dark moon and without power. However it is good for aggressive worship of ugra Devatas and tantric rituals |
| 16. | Purnima | None | ➢ It's Highly Auspicious and Moon is at its brightest and most Benefic status.<br>➢ Natives born in Purnima – attain great status and fame |

## 9. THITHI SHUNYA : Few More snapshots

1. We know that Thithi signifies the distance between Sun – the Eternal Atmakaraka &the Moon – The Physical Body & Mind. Amavasya is the Thithi, when Moon is deprived of the power to reflect the Sun light. Likewise Certain Signs of the Zodiac are stated to be deprived of this light/water from the Moon & and are stated to be in deficiency during the particular Thithi. They are designated as Thithi Shunya Rashis for Each Thithi.

2. The Zodiac Signs which are impacted due to the Particular Thithi's (indicated in Number) are tabulated in **Table – 2** for reference. The impact of Thithi Shunya is not uniform but varies wrt each ascendant & Bhava. This has been vastly misunderstood by many & various theories galore.

3. The easy way to understand its impact is facilitated by this chart – **Table 2**. The Rashis which gets impacted during certain Thithi's is mentioned therein.

4. Accordingly, we can infer – that those born in Cancer ASC/ Moon sign shall be affected by Saptami only and Likewise

Aquarius born – By Chathurthi Thithi and Taurus Born Natives – by Chathurthi & Trayodashi and so on.

**Simply put – The Thithi mentioned in the various signs of the zodiac – Rashi – are not favourable for the Concerned Ascendant/ Moon Sign born Natives**

| TABLE 2 | | | |
|---|---|---|---|
| Pisces 2,11,14 | Aries 6 | Taurus 4,13 | Gemini 5,8,14 |
| Aquarius 4 | Thithi Shunya – Rashiwise (The Number indicates the corresponding Thithi which gets Shunya(burnt) in that Rashi-Sign) | | Cancer 7 |
| Capricorn 1,3,12 | | | Leo 3,6,9,10,13 |
| Sagittarius 2,7,11,14 | Scorpio 9,10 | Libra 1,12 | Virgo 5,8,14 |

## 10. **Note: In Conclusion**

- ✓ Thithi Shunya (TS) is often just one of the compounding factors – not a very virulent one is a fact.
- ✓ This affects, mostly in the Matter of Progeny & that too when 5&8 are connected.
- ✓ TS, does not affect Material Significations-Also Karana Lord – neutralises the TS

**Hence, TS – Daghda Rashi, impact is very limited & mostly confines to Progeny problems and in Match Making.**

## 11. Material Prosperity of the Native – Through Thithi & Karana: Few Additional Pointers

1. The Panchanga in general is a veritable tool – in – aid to achieve some Dependable Derivations from a Natal chart. Thithi is the Primary Element of the Panchanga and A Karana is half of Thithi – which signifies the modifier impact of the Thithi.

2. In Short a Thithi signifies the Wealth of All kinds (16 types) promised in the chart & the means too. The Karana indicates how it is achieved – like the mode and means of one's activity – profession and possible success rate.

3. As discussed earlier, Karana is half of a Thithi – Which act as a modifier of Thithi Significations. Each Thithi has 4 Karanas – 2 each in each Paksha (fortnight). These 4 Karanas act as modifiers for deciphering the Thithi Significations in depth.

   ➢ Ex: The impact of Pratipada – Kinstughna combine is vastly different from Pratipada – Bava, Pratipada – Balava, Pratipada – Kaulava combinations for all those born under Pratipada Thithi.

4. We all know that the 5th Bhava signifies New Creation, Skill Set, Talent and Purva Punya. Sun, the Lord of 5H of the KPC and is the Soul behind all these creation. The Moon is the – Physical Body and Mind & all Jeevas are born on earth under their collective influence. Hence, the creation of wealth could be ascertained based on the movement of Sun & Moon in relation to each other & the possible associated Bhava of Moon from Sun – Keeping Sun as the Lagna. After all the source of wealth & Karma originate from their association (They signify our source of creation)

5. The relevant Bhava and Karana associated with each Thithi could be ascertained from the Moons position from the Sun. **In order to decipher our Source of Wealth & Activity – Profession we need to combine the Significations of our birth – Thithi, Associated Karana & Bhava as detailed to achieve pin pointed accuracy of our predictions. Thithi indicates the Source and Karana the action to achieve it.**

**Table – 1**

| S. NO | Sun-Moon (Degree) | Sukla Paksha Thithi | Karana linked to the Thithi | | Remarks |
|---|---|---|---|---|---|
| | | | 1st Half | 2nd Half | |
| 1. | 0-12 | Pratipada | Kinstughna | Bava | We have to infer the Prosperity & the means like Profession etc. by connecting the Thithi, karana and the Bhava(counted from Sun to Moon) as indicated in the table |
| 2. | 12-24 | Dwitiya | Balava | Kaulava | |
| 3. | 24-36 | Tritiya | Taitula | Garaja | |
| 4. | 36-48 | Chathurthi | Vanija | Bhadra | |
| 5. | 48-60 | Panchami | Bava | Balava | |
| 6. | 60-72 | Shashti | Kaulava | Taitula | |
| 7. | 72-84 | Saptami | Garaja | Vanija | |
| 8. | 84-96 | Ashtami | Bhadra | Bava | |
| 9. | 96-108 | Navami | Balava | Kaulava | |
| 10. | 108-120 | Dashami | Taitula | Garaja | |
| 11. | 120-132 | Ekadashi | Vanija | Bhadra | |
| 12. | 132-144 | Dwadashi | Bava | Balava | |
| 13. | 144-156 | Trayodashi | Kaulava | Taitula | |
| 14. | 156-168 | Chaturdashi | Garaja | Vanija | |
| 15. | 168-180 | Purnima | Bhadra | Bava | |

| S. NO | Sun-Moon (Degree) | Krishna Paksha Thithi | Karana linked to the Thithi | | Remarks |
|---|---|---|---|---|---|
| | | | 1st Half | 2nd Half | |
| 1. | 180-192 | Pratipada | Balava | Kaulava | |
| 2. | 192-204 | Dwitiya | Taitula | Garaja | |
| 3. | 204-216 | Tritiya | Vanija | Bhadra | |
| 4. | 216-228 | Chathurthi | Bava | Balava | |
| 5. | 228-240 | Panchami | Kaulava | Taitula | |
| 6. | 240-252 | Shashti | Garaja | Vanija | |
| 7. | 252-264 | Saptami | Bhadra | Bava | |
| 8. | 264-276 | Ashtami | Balava | Kaulava | |
| 9. | 276-288 | Navami | Taitula | Garaja | |
| 10. | 288-300 | Dashami | Vanija | Bhadra | |
| 11. | 300-312 | Ekadashi | Bava | Balava | |
| 12. | 312-324 | Dwadashi | Kaulava | Taitula | |
| 13. | 324-336 | Trayodashi | Garaja | Vanija | |
| 14. | 336-348 | Chaturdashi | Bhadra | Shakuni | |
| 15. | 348-360 | Amavasya | Chatushpada | Nagava | |

## 12. Classification and grouping of Thithi by classics

The Thithis are broadly classified into 5 groups as under with each classification signifying a particular outcome. Ex:Rikta Thithi are avoided for all activities etc.

| Classification and Grouping of Thithi by Classics (Thithi's are referred through Numbers) | | | | |
|---|---|---|---|---|
| Nanda | Bhadra | Jaya | Riktha | Poorna |
| 1 | 2 | 3 | 4 | 5 |
| 6 | 7 | 8 | 9 | 10 |
| 11 | 12 | 13 | 14 | 15/30 |
| Happiness-Ananda (Rise/Fame/ Happiness) | Healthy-Aroghya (Health/ friendly/Fame) | Victory-Jayam (Strength/ Conflict/ Victory) | Loss – Nashta (Negative/ Aggression /Loss) | Complete-Full-Sampurna (Wealth/Satvik) |
| Auspicious | | | INAUSPICIOUS | Auspicious |

| Table : Thithi & Karana connectivity in the sequence of their occurrence | | | | | | | |
|---|---|---|---|---|---|---|---|
| S. No | Thithi | Karana (Shukla Paksha) | | Karana (Krishna Paksha) | | Thithi Classification |
| 1. | Pratipada | Kinstughna | Bava | Balava | Kaulava | Nanda |
| 2. | Dwitiya | Balava | Kaulava | Taitula | Garaja | Bhadra |
| 3. | Tritiya | Taitula | Garaja | Vanija | Bhadra | Jaya |
| 4. | Chathurthi | Vanija | Bhadra | Bava | Balava | Riktha |
| 5. | Panchami | Bava | Balava | Kaulava | Taitula | Poorna |
| 6. | Shashti | Kaulava | Taitula | Garaja | Vanija | Nanda |
| 7. | Saptami | Garaja | Vanija | Bhadra | Bava | Bhadra |
| 8. | Ashtami | Bhadra | Bava | Balava | Kaulava | Jaya |
| 9. | Navami | Balava | Kaulava | Taitula | Garaja | Riktha |
| 10. | Dashami | Taitula | Garaja | Vanija | Bhadra | Poorna |
| 11. | Ekadashi | Vanija | Bhadra | Bava | Balava | Nanda |
| 12. | Dwadashi | Bava | Balava | Kaulava | Taitula | Bhadra |
| 13. | Trayodashi | Kaulava | Taitula | Garaja | Vanija | Jaya |
| 14. | Chaturdashi | Garaja | Vanija | Bhadra | Shakuni | Riktha |
| 15. | Amavasya | | | Chatushpada | Nagava | Poorna |
| 16. | Purnima | Bhadra | Bava | | | Poorna |

*Most Inauspicious

Note: The Mode of Acquisition of Material Wealth (Viz. the Activity-Profession) could be deciphered by linking the Respective Thithi and the linked Karana corresponding to that in the Birth time (Each Thithi has 4 Karanas in a Lunar Month)